Andrew Kippis, John Pringle

Six Discourses

Andrew Kippis, John Pringle

Six Discourses

ISBN/EAN: 9783337311056

Printed in Europe, USA, Canada, Australia, Japan

Cover: Foto ©Andreas Hilbeck / pixelio.de

More available books at **www.hansebooks.com**

SIX

DISCOURSES,

DELIVERED BY

Sir JOHN PRINGLE, Bart.

WHEN PRESIDENT OF THE

ROYAL SOCIETY;

On occasion of Six Annual Assignments of

SIR GODFREY COPLEY's MEDAL.

———————

TO WHICH IS PREFIXED THE

LIFE OF THE AUTHOR.

By ANDREW KIPPIS, D.D. F.R.S. and S.A.

———————

LONDON:

PRINTED FOR W. STRAHAN; AND T. CADELL,
IN THE STRAND.

M.DCC.LXXXIII.

PREFACE.

SOME time before Sir John Pringle's deceafe, feveral of his friends expreffed a wifh that he would collect into a volume the Six Difcourfes he had delivered, upon occafion of fo many annual affignments of Sir Godfrey Copley's Medal. This he declined doing, during his own life; but was difpofed to have them publifhed, in the manner that was requefted, after his death: for which exprefs purpofe, he committed a copy of them into my hands, a few days before he fet out for Edinburgh, in 1781. But, notwithftanding my authority from Sir John Pringle, as the Difcourfes had been originally printed

under

under the fanction, and by the command, of the Royal Society, I did not think myfelf juftified in republifhing them, without the permiffion of that learned Body. Accordingly, I applied to Sir Jofeph Banks, who took up the matter with great readinefs and politenefs ; and, laying it before the Council, it was unanimoufly agreed that I fhould have their confent and approbation in the execution of my defign. For the condefcenfion and favour thus obligingly fhewn to me, both by the Prefident and the Council, I here defire their acceptance of my grateful acknowledgments.

Many of the materials from which the following Narrative is compofed, have been furnifhed me by Sir John Pringle's family and friends. In this refpect, I am particularly obliged to

the

the attention and care of Sir James
Pringle, and Dr. Hope of Edinburgh.
Other circumftances have been collected from feveral gentlemen in London;
and efpecially from Dr. William Watfon, Dr. Richard Saunders, and Mr.
Stevenfon. With the latter part of our
Author's Life I was myfelf well acquainted; having been honoured with
his friendfhip for nearly ten years
before his deceafe. When the fucceeding Account of him had been
moft of it printed off, James Bofwell
Efq. was fo good as to favour me
with a recital of various particulars,
drawn from his own intimacy with
Sir John Pringle, and from the information of his father, Lord Auchinleck. This communication did not
come fo late, but that I was able to
avail myfelf of it, in feveral refpects.
Two things are mentioned by Mr.
Bofwell,

Bofwell, that I had not been informed of before ; and which, therefore, could not be introduced in their proper places. One is, that Sir John Pringle, after he had ftudied at the Univerfity of Edinburgh, was intended for the mercantile line, and that he went to Amfterdam for that purpofe; but that his mind was turned to Phyfic, by accidentally hearing, at Leyden, a lecture of Boerhaave's, which ftruck him in a remarkable manner. The other is, that he completed his medical ftudies at Paris. This I fufpected to be the cafe ; but not being affured of it, I did not choofe to infert it in my Narration. Where any circumftances are taken from books, I have referred to my authorities. It will be feen that I am under fome obligations to the Anecdotes of Mr. Bowyer, by my friend

Mr.

Mr. Nichols ; to whom Biography, and Biographers in general, are fo much indebted.

I defire the Reader to remember, that it hath been my intention to give a Life of Sir John Pringle, with plainnefs and fimplicity ; and not a ftudied panegyric. The elaborate and oratorical form of the profeffed Eulogium, which, on certain occafions, has its ufe and its beauty, I leave to the much abler men, who will undertake it at Paris ; and I fhall efteem. myfelf happy in having had it in my power to provide them with materials for their more elegant narratives. They may depend upon it, that Truth hath been my object ; and that I have faid nothing concerning Sir John Pringle, which, I believe, will not be acknowledged to be juft, by thofe who were beft acquainted with his character.

L I F E

O F

Sir JOHN PRINGLE, Bart.

SIR JOHN PRINGLE was born at Stichel-Houfe, in the county of Rox-burgh, North Britain, on the 10th of April, 1707. His father was Sir John Pringle of Stichel, Bart. and his mother, whofe name was Magdalen Eliott, was fifter to Sir Gilbert Eliott of Stobs, Bart. Both the families from which he defcended were very antient and honourable ones in the fouth of Scotland, and were in great efteem for their attachment to the religion and liberties of their country, and for their

a   piety

piety and virtue in private life. He was
the youngeft of feveral fons, three of
whom, befides himfelf, arrived to years of
maturity *. His grammatical education he
received

* Robert, the eldeft, fucceeded to the eftate and
title of the family, and died, not many years fince, at
an advanced age. Gilbert, the fecond, was an officer in the army; and Walter, the third, who was
brought up to the law, was Sheriff of the county of
Roxburgh. Sir John Pringle of Stichel had alfo,
by his Lady, an only daughter, Margaret, who
was married to Sir James Hall, Bart. of Dunglafs,
and was mother to the late Sir John, and grandmo-
ther to the prefent Sir James Hall. Robert Pringle,
Efq; a brother of the firft Sir John Pringle, having
quitted his native country, during the tyrannical government of King James the Second, came over with
the Prince of Orange at the Revolution, and was appointed Deputy Secretary of State for Scotland. He
was afterwards Secretary of War for Great Britain,
and, at length, Regifter General of the Shipping;
which poft he held till his deceafe. In Carftares's
State-Papers, there are five letters written by him,
which fhew that he was a fenfible and moderate man,
and well verfed in public affairs. He departed this
life at Rotterdam, on his return to England from the
Spa, on the 13th of September 1736, being eighty
years of age. Another brother of the firft Sir John
Pringle,

received at home, under a private tutor;
and after having made fuch a progrefs as
qualified him for academical ftudies, he
was removed to the univerfity of St.
Andrews, where he was put under the
immediate care of Mr. Francis Pringle,
profeffor of Greek in the college, and a
near relation of his father. Having continued here fome years, he went to Edinburgh, in October 1727, for the purpofe
of ftudying phyfic, that being the ¡profef-

Pringle, was Sir Walter Pringle, Knight, one of the
fenators of the college of juftice at Edinburgh, under the title of Lord Newhall. This gentleman was
eminently diftinguifhed by his abilities and virtues;
having been efteemed, in his time, as an ornament to
the bench and the profeffion of the law, and as the
pride and boaft of his family and country. A character was drawn of him by the late Lord Prefident
Arnifton, and publifhed in the Scots Magazine. He
died on the 13th of December, 1736; and an epitaph
was written on him by Hamilton of Bangour, which
is inferted in that Author's volume of poems. There
is, likewife, an engraved Portrait of Sir Walter
Pringle.

fion

lion which he was now determined to follow. At Edinburgh, however, he ftayed only one year, the reafon of which was, that he was defirous of going to Leyden, at that time the moft celebrated fchool of medicine in Europe. Dr. Boerhaave, who had fo eminently contributed to bring that univerfity into reputation, was confiderably advanced in years; and Mr. Pringle was unwilling, by delay, to expofe himfelf to the danger of lofing the benefit of that great man's Lectures. We need not fay that he here maintained the moft diligent application to his medical ftudies, and that he made the beft ufe of the inftructions given him by the illuftrious profeffor upon whom he attended. For Boerhaave he had a high and juft refpect: but it was not his difpo-fition and character to become the implicit and fyftematic follower of any man, how-ever able and diftinguifhed. Whilft he ftudied at Leyden, he contracted an inti-

mate

mate friendſhip with Van Swieten, who afterwards became ſo famous at Vienna, both by his practice and writings. Van Swieten was not only Mr. Pringle's acquaintance and fellow ſtudent at the univerſity, but alſo his phyſician, when he happened to be ſeized there with a fit of ſicknefs. Nevertheleſs, he did not owe his recovery to his friend's advice: for Van Swieten having refuſed to give him the bark, another preſcribed it, and Mr. Pringle was cured. When he had gone through his proper courſe of ſtudies at Leyden, he was admitted, on the 20th of July, 1730, to his Doctor of Phyſic's degree. His inaugural Diſſertation, which, according to cuſtom, was printed, was " de marcore ſenili;" and his diploma was ſigned, beſides the other profeſſors of the univerſity, by Boerhaave, Albinus, and Gravefande ; names of great celebrity, not

a 3   only

only in the medical world, but among the learned in general.

Upon quitting Leyden, Dr. Pringle fettled as a phyſician at Edinburgh, where he gained the eſteem of the magiſtrates of the city, and of the profeſſors of the college, by his abilities and good conduct. Though his ſtudies might principally be confined to his own profeſſion, this was not ſo entirely the caſe, but that he could find time for paying a conſiderable degree of attention to other objects, and particularly to thoſe highly important ones, natural religion and morality. Such, it is certain, was his known acquaintance with ethical ſubjects, that, on the 28th of March, 1734, he was appointed, by the magiſtrates and council of the city of Edinburgh, to be joint Profeſſor of Pneumatics and Moral Philoſophy with Mr. Scott, during the

ſaid

faid Mr. Scott's life, and fole Profeffor thereof after his deceafe; and, in confequence of this appointment, Dr. Pringle was admitted, on the fame day, a member of the univerfity. In difcharging the duties of this new employment, his text book was PUFFENDORFF *De Officio Hominis et Civis;* and agreeably to the method he purfued through life, of making fact and experiment the bafis of fcience, he recommended much to his pupils Lord Bacon's works, and particularly the *Novum Organum* of that Father of true Philofophy. Befides this, he annually delivered feveral lectures on the immateriality and immortality of the foul; fubjects that fell properly within his province, and which were not a little difcuffed at that period.

Dr. Pringle continued in the practice of phyfic at Edinburgh, and in performing

the

the obligations of his profefforfhip, till
1742, when he was appointed phyfician to
the Earl of Stair, who then commanded
the Britifh army. For this appointment
he was chiefly indebted to his friend Dr,
Stevenfon, an eminent phyfician at Edinburgh, who had an intimate acquaintance
with Lord Stair,

By the intereft of this nobleman, Dr,
Pringle was conftituted, on the 24th of Auguft 1742, phyfician to the military hofpital
in Flanders; and it was provided in the
commiffion, that he fhould receive a falary
of twenty fhillings a-day, and be entitled to
half pay for life. He did not, on this occafion, refign his profefforfhip of Moral
Philofophy. The univerfity permitted him
to retain it, and Meffrs. Muirhead and
Cleghorn were allowed to teach in his
abfence. The fame indulgence was granted
him,

him, from year to year, as long as he continued to requeſt it.

The eminent attention which Dr. Pringle paid to his duty as an army phyſician, is a matter that requires no enlargement in this place. It is a faĉt ſo generally known, and ſo univerſally acknowledged, that it cannot admit of a debate or a doubt ; and were there no other teſtimony, it would be amply apparent from every page of his Treatiſe on the Diſeaſes of the Army. One thing, however, deſerves particularly to be mentioned, as it is highly probable that it was owing to his ſuggeſtion. It had hitherto been uſual, for the ſecurity of the ſick, when the enemy was near, to remove them a great way from the camp ; the conſequence of which was, that many were loſt before they came under the care of the phyſicians. The Earl of Stair, being ſenſible of this evil, propoſed to the

Duke

Duke de Noailles, when the army was encamped at Afchaffenburg, in 1743, that the hofpitals on both fides fhould be confidered as fanctuaries for the fick, and mutually protected. The French general, who was diftinguifhed for his humanity, readily agreed to the propofal, and took the firft opportunity of fhewing a proper regard to his engagement. For, after the battle of Dettingen, when the Britifh hofpital was at Feckenheim, a village upon the Maine, at a diftance from the camp, the Duke de Noailles, having occafion to fend a detachment to another village upon the oppofite bank, and apprehending that this might alarm the fick, he fent to acquaint them, that he had given exprefs orders to his troops not to difturb them. This agreement was ftrictly obferved on both fides during that campaign *.

---

* Preface to the Obfervations on the Difeafes of the Army, p. 8. Seventh edition.

At

At the battle of Dettingen, Dr. Pringle was in a coach with Lord Carteret during the whole time of the engagement, and the fituation they were placed in was dangerous. They had been taken at unawares, and were kept betwixt the fire of the line in front, a French battery on the left, and a wood full of huffars on the right. The coach was occafionally fhifted, to avoid being in the eye of the battery.

Soon after this event, Dr. Pringle met with no fmall affliction in the retirement of his great friend, the Earl of Stair, from the army. He offered to refign with his noble patron : but that generous and liberal minded commander not permitting him to think of it for a moment, he was obliged to content himfelf with teftifying his refpect and gratitude to his Lordfhip, by accompanying him forty miles on his return

turn to England; after which he took leave
of him with the utmoſt regret.

But though Dr. Pringle was thus deprived of the immediate proteḍtion of a
nobleman who knew and eſteemed his
worth, his conduḍt in the duties of his
ſtation procured him effeḍtual ſupport.
He attended the army, in Flanders, through
the campaign of 1744, and ſo powerfully
recommended himſelf to the Duke of Cumberland, that, in the ſpring following, on
the 11th of March, he had a commiſſion
from his Royal Highneſs, appointing him
Phyſician General to his Majeſty's forces
in the Low Countries, and parts beyond
the ſeas: and on the next day he received
a ſecond commiſſion from the Duke, by
which he was conſtituted Phyſician to the
Royal hoſpitals in the ſame countries.

Hitherto Dr. Pringle had not been certain whether he might not find reaſon to
return

return to the duties of his ſtation at Edinburgh, and to his medical practice in that city. But no ſooner was he aſſured of the promotions we have juſt mentioned, than he thougbt proper to reſign his Profeſſorſhip of Pneumatics and Moral Philoſophy. His letter to this purpoſe, addreſſed to Dr. Wiſhart, Principal of the college, is dated on the 5th of March, 1744-5 ; in which, with many expreſſions of gratitude, reſpect, and affection to the univerſity, he declares that he gives up his charge without condition or limitation.

In 1745, he was with the army in Flanders, but was recalled from that country, in the latter end of the year, to attend the forces which were to be ſent againſt the Rebels in Scotland. At this time he had the honour of being choſen a Fellow of the Royal Society. The election was on the 30th of October, and the

9 .   *Society*

Society had reafon to be pleafed with the
addition of a member, who was earneftly
devoted to the purfuit of fcience in general,
and who had the reputation and intereft of
natural and experimental philofophy particularly at heart. How well he merited
the diftinction conferred upon him, will
hereafter appear.

Dr. Pringle, at the beginning of the
year 1746, accompanied, in his official
capacity, the Duke of Cumberland in his
expedition againft the Rebels, and remained with the forces, after the battle of
Culloden, till their return to England, in
the middle of Auguft. We do not find
that he was in Flanders during any part of
that year. In 1747 and 1748, he again
attended the army abroad; and in the
autumn of 1748, he embarked with the
forces for England, upon the conclufion of
the treaty of Aix la Chapelle. From that
time

time he principally refided in London, where, from his known fkill and experience, and the reputation he had acquired, he might reafonably expect to fucceed as a phyfician. It was to his knowledge, his application, and his attention alone, that he trufted for making his way in the metropolis. If any little artifices are ever made ufe of, in the city of London, to excite popularity, and to promote medical practice, Dr. Pringle was the laft man to adopt fuch artifices. If he could not have built his fuccefs on the bafis of fubftantial merit, he would not have fucceeded at all. We cannot but think that fuch a conduct is highly deferving of approbation and applaufe. In every profeffion of life, there is no fatisfaction that is equal to the confcioufnefs of inward worth, and of a mind fuperior to the various contrivances for obtaining the notice and favour of mankind

kind, to which infufficiency, vanity, or
covetoufnefs fometimes have recourfe.

In the month of April, 1749, Dr. Pringle
was appointed Phyfician in Ordinary to his
Royal Highnefs the Duke of Cumberland *. In 1750, he publifhed, in a letter
to Dr. Mead, " Obfervations on the
Jail or Hofpital Fever." This piece, which
paffed through two editions, and was occafioned by the jail-diftemper that broke
out at that time in the city of London, was
well received by the medical world, though
he himfelf afterwards confidered it as
having been haftily written. After fupplying fome things that were omitted, and
rectifying certain miftakes that were made
in it, he included it in his grand work on
the Difeafes of the Army, where it con-

* Gent. Mag. Vol. xix. p. 189.

ftitutes

ftitutes the feventh chapter of the third
part of that Treatife.

It was in the fame year, that Dr. Pringle
began to communicate to the Royal Society
his famous ' Experiments upon Septic and
' Antifeptic Subftances, with Remarks re-
' lating to their Ufe in the Theory of
' Medicine.' Thefe Experiments, which
comprehended feveral Papers, were read at
different meetings of the Society; the firft
in June, and the two next in the November following : three more in the courfe of
the year 1751 ; and the laft, in February,
1752. Only the three firft Numbers were
printed in the Philofophical Tranfactions ;
the reafon of which was, that Dr. Pringle
had fubjoined the whole, by way of Appendix, to his ' Obfervations on the Dif-
' eafes of the Army;' for it is a general rule
with the Royal Society, to infert, in their
Journals, none of thofe Papers which, having

b   been

been read before them, are afterwards publifhed by the Authors themfelves.

The Experiments upon Septic and Antifeptic Subftances, which haye accompanied every fubfequent edition of the treatife
juft mentioned, procured for cur ingenious
Phyfician the honour of Sir Godfrey Copley's gold medal. Befides this, they gained
him a high and juft reputation, as an experimental philofopher ; and, perhaps, have
not a little contributed to promote that ardent fpirit of enquiry into the chemical
powers and properties of Nature, which
hath lately been productive of fuch wonderful difcoveries.

But though the Papers now fpecified
were Dr. Pringle's chief communications to
the Royal Society ; the communications
that were the moft important in themfelves,
and on which his philofophical fame was
principally

principally founded; they were not the fole evidences of his folicitude, whilft only a private member of that learned Body, to carry on the purpofes of its inftitution. Not again to refume the fubject, we fhall here mention feveral inftances befides of his attention to Natural Knowledge, which have occurred to us, in looking over the Philo-fophical Tranfactions, and other publica-tions.

In February, 1753, he prefented to the Society an ' Account of feveral Perfons ' feized with the Gaol Fever by working ' in Newgate, and of the Manner by which ' the Infection was communicated to one ' entire Family.' This is a very curious Paper; and it was deemed of fuch import-ance by the excellent Dr. Stephen Hales, that he requefted the Author's permiffion to have it publifhed, for the common good of the kingdom, in the Gentleman's Maga-

b 2   zine;

zine; where it was accordingly printed, previoufly to its appearance in the Tranf-actions *. Dr. Pringle's next communication was, ' A remarkable Cafe of Fragility, ' Flexibility, and Diffolution of the Bones †.' In the forty-ninth volume of the Tranfac-tions, we meet with accounts which he had given of an earthquake felt at Bruffels; of another at Glafgow and Dunbarton ‡; and of the agitation of the waters, on the firft of November, 1756, in Scotland and at Hamburgh §. The fifteenth volume con-tains Obfervations, by him, on the Cafe of Lord Walpole, of Woolterton; and a Re-lation of the Virtues of Soap, in diffolving the Stone, as experienced by the Reverend

* Gentleman's Magazine, vol. xxiii. p. 71—74. Philofophical Tranfactions, vol. xlviii. part i. p. 42—54.

† Ibid. p. 297—301.

‡ The greater part of the Paper is by Dr. Whyt.

§ Vol. xlix. part ii. p. 509—511. 546, 547. 550, 551.

Mr.

Mr. Matthew Simfon *. The next volume is enriched with two of the Doctor's Articles, of confiderable length, as well as value. In the firft, he hath collected, digefted, and related the different accounts that had been given of a very extraordinary fiery meteor, which appeared on Sunday, the 26th of November 1758, between eight and nine at night; and, in the fecond, he hath made a variety of remarks upon the whole, wherein is difplayed no fmall degree of philofophical fagacity †. It would be tedious to mention the various Papers, which, both before and after he became Prefident of the Royal Society, were tranfmitted through his hands. The merit of thefe Papers muft principally and diftinctively reft with the Gentlemen by whom they were drawn up ; though there

* Vol. l. part. i. p. 205—209. 219. 221.

† Vol. li. part i. p. 218—274.

can

can be no doubt, but that fome of them
were prepared in confequence of his particular requeft, and might probably derive
a confiderable portion of their accuracy and
perfection from the hints which he had
fuggefted. Befides his communications in
the Philofophical Tranfactions, he wrote,
in the Edinburgh Medical Effays, volume
the fifth, an Account of the Succefs of the
Vitrum ceratum Antimonii.

On the 14th of April, 1752, Dr. Pringle
married Charlotte, the fecond daughter of
Dr. Oliver, an eminent phyfician at Bath,
and who had long been at the head of his
profeffion in that city. This connection
did not laft long; the lady dying in the
fpace of a few years.

Nearly about the time of his marriage,
Dr. Pringle gave to the Public the firft edition

tion of his ' Obfervations on the Difeafes
' of the Army.' It was reprinted, in the
year following, with fome additions. To
the third edition, which was greatly improved from the farther experience the
Author had gained by attending the camps,
for three feafons, in England, an Appendix
was annexed, in anfwer to fome remarks
that Profeffor De Haen, of Vienna, and
M. Gaber, of Turin, had made on the
Work. The like attention was paid to the
improvement of the Treatife, in every fubfequent edition. From more mature reflection, from the additional experience
afforded by his private practice, and from
his intercourfe with the medical gentlemen
who had been employed in the hofpitals
abroad, in different climates, during the
late war,—Dr. Pringle had an opportunity
of expreffing, with greater confidence, fome
of his former obfervations; and of omitting others, which he had advanced with-

out

out fufficient foundation. The work is divided into three parts; the firft of which, being principally hiftorical, may be read with pleafure by every gentleman. The latter parts lie more within the province of phyficians. They alone are the beft judges of the merit of the performance; and to its merit the moft decifive and ample teftimonies have been given. It hath gone through feven editions at home; and, abroad, it has been tranflated into the French, the German, and the Italian languages. Scarcely any medical writer hath mentioned it, without fome tribute of applaufe. Ludwig, in the fecond volume of his ‘ Commentarii ‘ de Rebus in Scientia Naturali et Medi- ‘ cina geftis,’ fpeaks of it highly; and gives an account of it, which comprehends fixteen pages. The celebrated and eminent Baron Van Haller, in his Bibliotheca Ana-tomica *, with a particular reference to the

---

* Tom. ii. p. 235.

treatife

treatife we are fpeaking of, ftiles the author
' Vir illuftris — de omnibus bonis artibus
' benè meritus,'

It would be eafy to produce a number
of encomiums of a fimilar kind; but it is
the lefs neceffary to multiply them, as the
excellence of Dr. Pringle's Work is fo generally acknowledged. It is allowed to be
a claffical book in the phyfical line; and
that it hath placed the Writer of it in a
rank with the famous Sydenham. Like
Sydenham, too, he hath become eminent,
not by the quantity, but the value of his
productions; and hath afforded a happy
inftance of the great and deferved fame,
which may fometimes arife from a fingle
performance. If it would not carry us too
far out of our way, it might be an amufing
fpeculation, to confider the different paths
which great men have purfued in their
literary courfe; and how happily fome few,

both

both among the ancients and the moderns, have attained a high degree of glory, by only one, or, at leaft, a fmall number of compofitions.

The reputation that Dr. Pringle gained by his ' Obfervations on the Difeafes of ' the Army,' was not of a kind which is ever likely to diminifh. He was happy in the choice of his fubject, which, though it ought long ago to have been completely handled, had fcarcely hitherto been touched upon ; and, though improvements will, no doubt, be made, and perhaps have been made, in the courfe of practice, as medical knowledge becomes more and more cultivated, the Work will always be held in efteem, as having been founded on the folid bafis of experience, and not of theory. Its fate will be very different from that of many fyftems, which, though they have raifed the fabricators of them to a

great

great temporary celebrity, have fpeedily funk into oblivion, if not into contempt. Various inftances might be mentioned of perfons, whofe hypothefes, notwithftanding their having been the applaufe and wonder of their day, are now, if not forgotten, totally difregarded. But we have no defign of exalting our Author by other men's difgrace.

The utility of Dr. Pringle's Treatife was of ftill greater importance than its reputation. From the time that he was appointed a Phyfician to the Army, it feems to have been his grand objeÉt, to leffen, as far as lay in his power, the calamities of war: nor was he without confiderable fuccefs in his noble and benevolent defign. It cannot be doubted, but that the treatment he hath recommended, from his own obfervation and experience, hath been adopted by the able and judicious praÉtitioners who have

fucceeded

fucceeded him; and that hence many lives have been preferved, which would other-wife have been loft to the community.

The benefits which may be derived from our Author's Obfervations on the Difeafes of the Army, are not folely confined to gentlemen of the medical profeffion. Com-manders may learn from them, and efpe-cially from the concluding chapter of the fecond part of the Treatife, to determine, with fome degree of certainty, what force may, at any time, be relied upon for fer-vice; the effects of fhort or long campaigns upon the health of the foldiers; the difference between taking the field early, and going late into winter quarters; with other calcula-tions, founded upon fuch materials as are furnifhed by war. General Melville, a gentleman who unites with his military abilities, the fpirit of philofophy, and the fpirit of humanity, was enabled, when

Governor

Governor of the Neutral Iflands, to be fingularly ufeful, in confequence of the inftructions he had received from Dr. Pringle's book, and from perfonal converfation
with him. By taking care to have his men
always lodged in large, open, and airy
apartments; and by rapidly fhifting their
quarters from the low, damp, and marfhy
parts of the country, to the dry and hilly
grounds, fo as never to let his forces remain long enough in the fwampy places,
to be injured by the noxious air of fuch
places, the General was the happy inftrument of faving the lives of feven hundred
foldiers. A more honourable teftimony
cannot be given to the utility of the principles and rules which had been laid down
by our Author.

In 1753, Dr. Pringle was chofen one of
the Council of the Royal Society. Though
he had not, for fome years, been called
abroad,

abroad, he ftill held his place of Phyfician to the Army; and, in the war that began in 1755, attended the camps, in England, during three feafons. This enabled him, from farther experience, to correct fome of his former obfervations, and to give additional perfection to the third edition of his great Work. In 1758, he entirely quitted the fervice of the Army; and being now determined to fix wholly in London, he was admitted a Licentiate of the College of Phyficians, on the fifth of July, in the fame year. The reafon why this matter was fo long delayed, might probably be, his not having hitherto come to a final refolution, with regard to his fettlement in the Metropolis.

After the acceffion of King George the Third to the throne of Great Britain, Dr. Pringle was appointed, in 1761, Phyfician to the Queen's Houfchold; and this honour

nour was fucceeded, by his being conftituted, in 1763, Phyfician Extraordinary to her
Majefty. On the twelfth of April, in the fame
year, he had been chofen a Member of the
Academy of Sciences at Haarlem ; and, on
the twenty-fifth of June following, he was
elected a Fellow of the Royal College of
Phyficians, London. In the fucceeding
November, he was returned on the ballot,
a fecond time, one of the Council of the
Royal Society ; and, in 1764, on the deceafe of Dr. Wollafton, he was made Phyfician in Ordinary to the Queen. On the
thirteenth of February 1766, he was
elected a foreign member, in the phyfical
line *, of the Royal Society of Sciences at
Goettingen ; and, on the fifth of June, in
that year, his Majefty was gracioufly pleafed
to teftify his fenfe of Dr. Pringle's abilities
and merit, by raifing him to the dignity of
a Baronet of Great Britain.

* Collega exterus Claffis Phyficæ.

On

On the eighteenth of July 1768, Sir
John Pringle was appointed Phyſician in
Ordinary to her late Royal Highneſs the
Princeſs Dowager of Wales; to which office a ſalary was annexed of one hundred
pounds a year. In 1770, he was choſen,
a third time, into the Council of the Royal
Society; as he was, likewiſe, a fourth time,
for the year 1772. Upon the thirtieth of
November, in that year, in conſequence of
the death of James Weſt Eſquire *, he was
elected

* James Weſt Eſq. had ſucceeded the Earl of
Morton, as Preſident of the Society. He was the ſon
of Richard Weſt Eſquire; and is underſtood to have
been deſcended from Thomas Weſt, Lord Delawar,
who lived in the reign of King James the Firſt. Mr.
James Weſt was educated at Baliol College, Oxford;
where he was admitted to the degree of Maſter of
Arts, on the twenty-third of June, 1726. In 1741,
he was choſen Repreſentative of the Borough of St.
Albans; which borough he continued to ſerve, during
ſeveral parliaments. Being appointed one of the
Joint Secretaries of the Treaſury, he remained in that
office many years; having held it till 1762. When,
in 1765, his old friend and patron, the Duke of New-
caſtle,

elected prefident of that illuftrious and
learned Body. His election to this high
ftation, though he had fo refpectable a

caftle, reverted to fome degree of power, by being
conftituted, during the fhort period of the Rockingham
adminiftration, Lord Privy Seal, his Grace obtained
for him an annual penfion of two thoufand pounds.
Mr. Weft was an early member of the Society of
Antiquaries, and at length one of its Vice-Prefidents.
Having been chofen a Fellow of the Royal Society,
he became, in a courfe of time, Treafurer to that
Body; and, at laft, as we have already feen, was
raifed to the Chair. Though he was a man of general learning, we do not recollect that he was eminently diftinguifhed by his acquaintance with Philofophical or Natural Knowledge. It admits of no doubt,
that, in this refpect, he was greatly excelled by moft of
the Prefidents who went before him, and by thofe who
were his fucceffors. As a Collector, he had great merit.
He had a large and valuable collection of manufcripts
relative to the Hiftory of England, which was fold,
after his deceafe, to the Earl of Shelburne. His
books, his prints and drawings, his coins and medals,
his pictures, and other mifcellaneous articles and cu-
riofities, were all of them difpofed of by auction, in
1773 : and the fale of the whole employed fifty-five
days. Mr. Weft died on the fecond of July,
1772. (Nichols's Anecdotes of Mr. Bowyer, p. 101,
102.)

c · character,

character, as the late Sir James Porter, for his opponent, was carried by a very confiderable majority. This was undoubtedly the higheft honour that Sir John Pringle ever received; an honour with which his other literary diftinctions could not be compared. He was fully fenfible of the eminent mark of efteem which the Royal Society had conferred upon him; and he was, at the fame time, deeply convinced, that his new fituation was not only a fituation of dignity, but of the greateft truft and importance. Accordingly, it was his determination to difcharge the duties of it with all the attention, affiduity, and zeal, of which he was capable.

It was at a very aufpicious time that Sir John Pringle was called upon to prefide over the Royal Society. A wonderful ardour for philofophical fcience, and for the advancement

ment of Natural Knowledge, had, of late
years, difplayed itfelf through Europe, and
had appeared with particular advantage in
our own country. Britons, to fay the leaft
of them, had had their full fhare in the difcoveries of magnetifm and electricity, in
botanical enquiries and refearches, and in
the purfuit of other important objects.
The fpirit of experimental inveftigation
into every part and property of Nature,
was high; and nothing could be more
agreeable to the genius of Sir John Pringle,
than to cherifh fuch a fpirit. He endeavoured to do it by all the methods that were
in his power; and he happily ftruck upon
a new way to diftinction and ufefulnefs, by
the difcourfes which were delivered by him
on the annual affignment of Sir Godfrey
Copley's Medal.

This gentleman had originally bequeathed five guineas, to be given, at each anni-

verfary

verfary meeting of the Royal Society, by
the determination of the Prefident and
Council, to the perfon who had been the
author of the beft Paper of Experimental
Obfervations for the year paft. In procefs
of time, this pecuniary reward, which
could never be an important confideration
to a man of an enlarged and philofophical
mind, however narrow his circumftances
might be, was changed into the more liberal form of a gold medal; in which form
it is become a truly honourable mark of
diftinction, and a juft and laudable object
of ambition. It was, no doubt, always
ufual with the Prefident, on the delivery of
the Medal, to pay fome compliment to the
gentleman on whom it was beftowed; but
the cuftom of making a fet fpeech on the
occafion, and of entering into the hiftory
of that part of philofophy to which the
experiments related, was firft introduced by
Mr. Martin Folkes. The Difcourfes, how-

2   ever,

ever, which he and his fucceffors delivered, were very fhort, and were only inferted in the minute-books of the Society. None of them had ever been printed before Sir John Pringle was raifed to the Chair. The firft fpeech that was made by him being much more elaborate and extended than ufual, the publication of it was defired ; and with this requeft it is faid that he was the more ready to comply, as an abfurd account of what he had delivered had appeared in a newfpaper.

Sir John Pringle was very happy in the fubject of his primary Difcourfe. The difcoveries in magnetifm and electricity had been fucceeded by the enquiries into the various fpecies of air. In thefe enquiries, Dr. Prieftley, who had already greatly diftinguifhed himfelf by his electrical experiments, and his other philofophical purfuits and labours, took the principal lead. A

Paper

Paper of his, entitled, ' Obfervations on ' different Kinds of Air,' having been read before the Society in March 1772, was adjudged to be deferving of the Gold Medal; and Sir John Pringle embraced with pleafure the occafion of celebrating the important communications of his Friend, and of relating, with accuracy and fidelity, what had previoufly been difcovered upon the fubject. At the clofe of the fpeech, he earneftly requefted Dr. Prieftley to continue his liberal and valuable enquiries; and we need not fay how eminently he hath fulfilled this requeft. The aftonifhing difcoveries he hath fince made, and is ftill making, have fet his name far above all praife.

It was not, we believe, intended, when Sir John Pringle's firft fpeech was printed, that the example fhould be followed: but the fecond Difcourfe was fo well received

by

by the Royal Society, that the publication of it was unanimoufly requefted. Both the Difcourfe itfelf, and the fubject on which it was delivered, merited fuch a diftinction. The compofition of the fecond fpeech is evidently fuperior to that of the former one; Sir John having probably been animated by the favourable reception of his firft effort. His account of the Torpedo, and of Mr. Walfh's ingenious and admirable experiments relative to the electrical properties of that extraordinary fifh, is fingularly curious. The whole Difcourfe abounds with ancient and modern learning, and exhibits Sir John Pringle's knowledge in Natural Hiftory, as well as in Medicine, to great advantage.

The third time that he was called upon to difplay his abilities at the delivery of Sir Godfrey Copley's Medal, was on an eminently beautiful and important occafion.

c 4

This

This was no lefs than Mr. (now Dr.) Mafkelyne's fuccefsful attempt completely to
eftablifh Sir Ifaac Newton's fyftem of the
univerfe, by his ' Obfervations made on
' the Mountain Schehallien, for finding its
' Attraction.' Sir John Pringle laid hold
of this opportunity to give a perfpicuous
and accurate relation of the feveral hypothefes of the ancients, with regard to the
revolutions of the heavenly bodies, and of
the noble difcoveries with which Copernicus enriched the aftronomical world. He
then traces the progrefs of the grand principle of Gravitation, down to Sir Ifaac's
illuftrious confirmation of it ; to which he
adds a concife narrative of Meffrs. Bouguer's and Condamine's experiment at
Chimboraco, and of Mr. Mafkelyne's at
Schehallien. If any doubts ftill remained,
with refpect to the truth of the Newtonian
Syftem, they are now totally removed. Dr.
Mafkelyne, who has otherwife largely contributed

tributed to the advancement of philofophical fcience, hath had the fingular honour
of eftablifhing fo firmly the doctrine of
univerfal attraction by this finifhing ftep of
analyfis, that the moft fcrupulous can no
longer hefitate to embrace a principle that
gives life to aftronomy, by accounting for
the various motions and appearances of the
hofts of heaven.

Sir John Pringle had reafon to be peculiarly fatisfied with the fubject of his fourth
Difcourfe ; that fubject being perfectly con-
genial to his difpofition and ftudies. His
own life had been much employed in
pointing out the means which tended not
only to cure, but to prevent, the difeafes
of mankind ; and it is probable, from his
intimate friendfhip with Captain Cook, that
he might fuggeft to that fagacious commander fome of the rules which he followed, in order to preferve the health of the

crew of his Majesty's ship the Refolution, during her voyage round the world. Whether this was the cafe, or whether the method purfued by the Captain, to attain fo falutary an end, was the refult alone of his own reflections, the fuccefs of it was aftonishing. Captain Cook, with a company of an hundred and eighteen men, performed a voyage of three years and eighteen days, throughout all the climates, from fifty-two degrees North to feventy-one degrees South, with the lofs of only one man by ficknefs. By precautions equally wife and fimple, he rendered the circumnavigation of the globe, fo far as health is concerned, quite a harmlefs object. It is no wonder that Sir John Pringle fhould celebrate, with affection, the conduct of his friend; who, befides his admirable fkill in preferving the lives and health of his failors, had not only difcovered, but furveyed, vaft tracts of new coafts; had difpelled the

illufion

illufion of a *Terra Auſtralis Incognita*, and
fixed the bounds of the habitable earth, as
well as thofe of the navigable ocean, in the
Southern hemifphere. Indeed, no one
could be more juſtly entitled to applaufe
than that man, who, independently of his
other claims to diſtinction, had been able,
by the practice of a few plain rules, refulting from the union of good fenfe, humanity, and experience, to render himfelf an
eminent benefactor to his fellow-creatures.
Captain Cook was not prefent to receive
the honour of the Gold Medal. He was
gone out upon the voyage from which he
never returned. In this laft voyage, he
was equally fuccefsful in maintaining the
health of his men ; and he determined the
point, which had fo long been contefted,
whether there is a practicable North-Weft
paffage from Europe to the Eaft Indies.
But though, in thefe refpects, he attained
the objects he had in view, it muft ever be
reflected

reflected upon with regret, that, in an unfortunate quarrel with the inhabitants of a
remote ifland, the world was deprived of
this great navigator, whofe excellence and
fame will be tranfmitted to the lateft pofterity.

Sir John Pringle, in his next annual dif-
fertation, had an opportunity of difplaying
his knowledge in a way in which it had
not hitherto appeared. The Difcourfe took
its rife from the Prize Medal's being adjudged to Mr. Mudge, then an eminent
furgeon at Plymouth, upon account of his
valuable Paper, containing directions for
making the beft compofition for the metals
of reflecting telefcopes, together with a de-
fcription of the procefs for grinding, polifh-
ing, and giving the great fpeculum the
true parabolic form. Sir John hath accurately related a variety of particulars, concerning the invention of reflecting telefcopes,

fcopes, the fubfequent improvements of thefe inftruments, and the ftate in which Mr. Mudge found them, when he firft fet about working them to a greater perfection, till he had truly realized the expectation of Sir Ifaac Newton, who, above an hundred years ago, prefaged that the Public would one day poffefs a parabolic fpeculum, not accomplifhed by mathematical rules, but by mechanical devices. From this narration our Author naturally rifes, in his thoughts, to the wonders that aftronomy prefents to our view, and to the admirable advantages which philofophical fcience hath derived from the methods that have been purfued for enlarging the powers of vifion.

It is impoffible to pafs over the fubject before us, without reflecting on the great acceffion which has been made to aftronomical knowledge, and the honour of the Society, fince Sir John Pringle was Prefi-dent.

dent. Every reader will immediately underftand that I refer to the communications of Mr. Herfchel; who hath carried
the magnifying power of telefcopes to a
height far beyond what had hitherto been
expected; who hath brought to light a
large number of double and triple ftars;
and who hath not only difcovered, but
afcertained without controverfy, the exiftence of a new primary planet, beyond
the orbit of Saturn, in the Solar Syftem;
to which, in honour of his Royal Patron
and Benefactor, he hath given the appel-
lation of the *Georgium Sidus.*

Sir John Pringle's fixth Difcourfe, to
which he was led by the affignment of the
Gold Medal to Mr. (now Dr.) Hutton, on
account of his curious Paper, entitled,
' The Force of fired Gun-powder, and
' the initial velocity of Cannon-balls, de-

I   ' termined

' termined by Experiments,' was on the theory of Gunnery. Though Sir John had fo long attended the army, this was probably a fubject to which he had heretofore paid very little attention. We cannot, however, help admiring with what perfpicuity and judgment he hath ftated the progrefs that was made, from time to time, in the knowledge of Projectiles, and the fcientific perfection to which his friend, Mr. Hutton, had carried this knowledge. As Sir John Pringle was not one of thofe who delighted in war, and in the fhedding of human blood, he was happy in being able to fhew, that even the ftudy of Artillery might be ufeful to mankind ; and, therefore, this is a topic which he hath not forgotten to mention.

Here ended our Author's Difcourfes upon the delivery of Sir Godfrey Copley's Medal. If he had continued to prefide in
the

the Chair of the Royal Society, he would,
no doubt, have found other occafions of
difplaying his acquaintance with the hiftory
of philofophy. But the opportunities
which he had of fignalizing himfelf in this
refpect, were important in themfelves,
happily varied, and fufficient to gain him
a folid and lafting reputation. Perhaps it
would not be defirable that publications
of fuch a nature fhould be very numerous;
fince, by that means, they might lofe, by
degrees, their novelty, their utility, and
their acceptance. We do not, therefore,
think that, in this particular view, Sir John
Pringle ought to be confidered as a model
to his fucceffors. It is beft that each Prefident fhould diftinguifh himfelf in that
way which is peculiarly fuited to his own
purfuits and ftudies; for thus, every
valuable object being regarded in its
turn, the honour of the Society, and
the interefts of philofophical and natural
knowledge,

knowledge, will moſt effectually be promoted.

The merit of the Papers that were communicated to the Royal Society, whilſt Sir
John Pringle prefided over it, was not confined to thoſe alone which were honoured
with the aſſignment of the Gold Medal.
Many of the Members diſtinguiſhed themfelves in the fame period, as is evident
from a furvey of the Tranfactions; and
many names might be mentioned with ap-
plauſe: but it would carry us far out of our
way to fpecify all of them; and it would
be too delicate a taſk, to fingle out fome
few, to the excluſion of others. Indeed,
the profperous ſtate in which the Royal
Society has long fubfifted, and in which it
continues to fubfift, muſt be reflected upon
with pleaſure by every lover of philofophical fcience.

d   Several

Several marks of literary diftinction, as we have already feen, had been conferred upon Sir John Pringle, before he was raifed to the Prefident's Chair. But, after that event, they were beftowed upon him in great abundance: and, not again to refume the fubject, I fhall here collect them together.

Previoufly, however, to thefe honours (excepting his having been chofen a Fellow of the Society of Antiquaries, London), he received the laft promotion that was given him in his medical capacity; which was, his being appointed, on the fourteenth of November, 1774, Phyfician Extraordinary to his Majefty. In the year 1776, he was enrolled in the lift of the members of no lefs than four learned Bodies. Thefe were, the Royal Academy of Sciences at Madrid; the Society, at Amfterdam, for the Promotion of Agriculture; the Royal Academy

Academy of Medical Correfpondence at Paris; and the Imperial Academy of Sciences at St. Peterfburgh. The times of Sir John Pringle's election into thefe eminent focieties, according to the order in which I have mentioned them, were on the twelfth of February, in the month of September, and on the twenty-eighth and twenty-ninth of December. Upon the laft occafion, he was honoured with the following Letter from Monfieur Euler; which hath been felected, out of many others of a fimilar nature, as an evidence of the regard and efteem wherein he was held by eminent foreigners.

' MONSIEUR,

' L' Academie Imperiale des Sciences
' vient de vous recevoir au nombre
' des fes Affociés étrangers, elle a voulù
' vous donner par là, Monfieur, un té-

' moignage public du grand cas qu'elle fait
' déja dépuis long tems des vos travaux, et
' que vous meritez à tant de titres. Mais
' ce que réleve encore d'avantage cette re-
' ception, et ce qui eft une diftinction trop
' marqué pour ne pas vous en faire l'ob-
' fervation, c'eft que votre aggregation a
' été proclamée le jour de l'affemblée fo-
' lemnelle, par laquelle l'Academie a céle-
' bré fon premier jubilé demi-féculaire,
' jour qu'elle mettra toujours au nombre
' de plus glorieux pour elle, par l'infigne
' faveur de fa Majefté le Roi de Pruffe, et
' de fon Alteffe Imperial Monfeigneur le
' Grand Duc, qui ont bien voulû con-
' fentir, qu'on les aggregeat à cette com-
' pagnie.

' Je m'applaudis d'être dans ce moment
' chargé de vous annoncer, Monfieur, cette
' nouvelle ; et je faifis, avec empreffement,
' une occafion auffi favorable de voux ex-
' primer

' primer les fentiments de la plus parfaite
' confidération, avec lefquels j'ai l'honneur
' d'être, Monfieur,

' Votre, &c.

(Signed) ' JEAN ALBERT EULER *.'

St. Peterfburgh,
Jan. 10, 1777.

On

* SIR,

' THE Imperial Academy of Sciences, being de-
' firous of giving a public teftimony of the high
' efteem which it has for your learned labours, and of
' its fenfe of your fervices to the republic of letters,
' hath admitted you into the number of its foreign
' Members. Your reception into this Body has alfo
' been diftinguifhed by one circumftance, too remark-
' able, and too honourable for you, to efcape obferva-
' tion. Your admiffion was publicly announced on a
' day of peculiar folemnity; on the day in which the
' Academy celebrated its firft jubilee, on account of
' its having fubfifted half a century ; and, at the fame
' time, when the Academy had the honour of re-
' ceiving into the number of its Members his Majefty
' the King of Pruffia, and his Imperial Highnefs the
' Grand Duke.

' I am extremely happy, Sir, to be appointed to
' communicate to you this information ; and gladly

d 3   ' embrace

On the fifth of July, 1777, Sir John
Pringle was nominated, by his Serene
Highnefs the Landgrave of Heffe, an honorary Member of the Society of Antiquaries at Caffel. In 1778, he fucceeded
the celebrated Linnæus, as one of the foreign Members of the Royal Academy of
Sciences at Paris. This honour is extended
by that illuftrious Body only to eight
perfons, on which account it is juftly
efteemed a moft eminent mark of diftinction ; and we believe there have been few
or no inftances, wherein it hath been conferred on any other than men of great and
acknowledged abilities and reputation. On
the eleventh of October, in the fame year,
our Author was chofen a Member of the
Medical Society at Hanau. In the fucceed-

‘ embrace this favourable opportunity of expreffing
‘ thofe fentiments of the moft perfect regard, with
‘ which I have the honour to be, Sir,

St. Peterfburgh,   Your &c.
Jan. 10, 1777.   JEAN ALBERT EULER.

ing

ing year, on the twenty-ninth of March,
he was elected a foreign Member of the
Royal Academy of Sciences and Belles
Lettres at Naples. The laft teftimony of
refpect which was, in this way, beftowed
upon Sir John Pringle, was his being admitted, in 1781, into the number of the
Fellows of the newly erected Society of
Antiquaries at Edinburgh. The particular
defign of the Society is to inveftigate the
Hiftory and Antiquities of Scotland: and,
from the known characters and literature
of the gentlemen who compofe it, there
can be little doubt, but that the end they
have in view will fuccefsfully be accomplifhed. Of this there is the greater reafon
to be confident, as I underftand, with
pleafure, that the deftruction of the Scottifh
records, by the cruel policy of king Edward
the Firft, was not fo univerfal, or fo general, as hath commonly been fuppofed.

d 4   It

It was at a late period of life, when Sir
John Pringle was in the fixty-fixth year of
his age, that he was chofen to be Prefident
of the Royal Society. Confidering, therefore, the extreme attention that was paid
by him to the various and important duties
of his office, and the great pains he took
in the preparation of his Difcourfes, it was
natural to expect that the burthen of his
honourable ftation fhould grow heavy upon
him in a courfe of time. This burthen
was increafed not only by the weight of
years, but by the accident of a fall in the
area of the back part of his houfe, from
which he received confiderable hurt, and
which, in its confequences, affected his
health, and weakened his fpirits. Such
being the ftate of his body and mind, he
began to entertain thoughts of refigning
the Prefident's Chair. It hath been faid
likewife, and believed, that he was much
hurt by the difputes introduced into the
Society,

Society, concerning the queſtion, whether
pointed or blunted electrical conductors are
the moſt efficacious in preſerving buildings
from the pernicious effects of lightning.
Of this matter the preſent Writer of his
Life can aſſert nothing from perſonal
knowledge : for though he was then in the
habit of a ſtrict intimacy with Sir John
Pringle, he never heard from him any
ſuggeſtion of the kind that has been mentioned. Perhaps Sir John Pringle's de-
clining years, and the general ſtate of his
health, will form ſufficient reaſons for his
reſignation. His intention, however, was
diſagreeable to many of his friends, and to
many diſtinguiſhed Members of the Royal
Society. Accordingly, they earneſtly ſoli-
cited him to continue in the Chair; but,
his reſolution being fixed, he reſigned it at
the Anniverſary Meeting in 1778. Joſeph
Banks Eſq. (now Sir Joſeph Banks, Bart.)
was unanimouſly elected Preſident in his
room ;

room; a gentleman in the prime and vigour of his life, who had eminently diftinguifhed himfelf by his acquaintance with Natural Hiftory; who had failed round the globe, and performed other voyages, in purfuit of that branch of fcience; who is preparing, at an immenfe expence and labour, the nobleft and moft fplendid botanical Work, which hath ever been prefented to the Public; and who hath amply juftified the choice that was made of him, by his attention to every part of his duty, and his affiduous concern to promote the intereft and honour of the Society.

Though Sir John Pringle quitted his particular relation to the Royal Society, and did not attend its meetings fo conftantly as he had formerly done, he ftill retained his literary connections in general. His houfe continued to be the refort of

ingenious

ingenious and philofophical men, whether
of his own country, or from abroad ; and
he was frequent in his vifits to his friends.
He was held in particular efteem by eminent and learned foreigners, none of whom
came to England without waiting upon
him, and paying him the greateſt refpeᴄt.
He treated them, in return, with diſtinguiſhed civility and regard. When a number of gentlemen met at his table, foreigners were uſually a part of the company ;
and it would have been an uncommon
thing not to have feen fome of them at his
Sunday evening converſations. I remember well, that, one night, the perfons prefent, being eight in number, were each of
them of a different nation ; if Sir John
Pringle, a Scotchman, and myfelf, an Eng-
liſhman, could be fo confidered. The fix
others confiſted of a Dutchman, a German, a Frenchman, a Spaniard, an Italian,
and a Ruffian. Though we were thus di-
verfified

verſified in country, education, modes of life, and principles of religion, no obſtructions hence aroſe to mutual harmony, pleaſure, and improvement.

Sir John Pringle's infirmities increaſing, he hoped that he might receive an advantage from an excurſion to Scotland, and ſpending the ſummer there; which he did in the year 1780, and principally at Edinburgh. He had probably then formed ſome deſign of fixing his reſidence in that city. However this may have been, he was ſo well pleaſed with a place to which he had been habituated in his younger days, and with the reſpect ſhewn him by his friends, that he purchaſed a houſe there, whither he intended to return in the following ſpring. When he came back to London, in the Autumn of the year above mentioned, he ſet about preparing to put his ſcheme in execution. Accordingly, having

having firft difpofed of the greateft part of his library, he fold his houfe in Pall-Mall, in April, 1781, and fome few days after removed to Edinburgh. In this city he was treated, by perfons of all ranks, with every mark of diftinc-tion. But Edinburgh was not now to him what it had been in early life. The vivacity of fpirits, which, in the days of youth, fpreads fuch a charm on the objects that furround us, was fled. Many, if not moft, of Sir John Pringle's old friends and contemporaries, were dead; and, though fome of them remained, they could not meet together with the fame ftrength of conftitution, the fame ardour of purfuit, the fame animation of hope, which they had formerly poffeffed. The younger men of eminence paid him the fincereft teftimonies of efteem and regard; but it was too late in life for him to form new habits of clofe and intimate friendfhip. He found, like-wife,

wife, the air of Edinburgh too fharp and
cold for his frame, which had long been
peculiarly fenfible to the feverities of weather. Thefe evils were exaggerated by his
increafing infirmities, and, perhaps, by
that reftleffnefs of mind, which, in the
midft of bodily complaints, is ftill hoping
to derive fome benefit from a change of
place. He determined, therefore, to return once more to London, where he arrived in the beginning of September.

Before Sir John Pringle entirely quitted
Edinburgh, he requefted his friend, Dr.
John Hope, to prefent ten volumes, folio,
of Medical and Phyfical Obfervations, in
manufcript, to the Royal College of Phyficians in that city. This benefaction was
conferred on two conditions; firft, that the
Obfervations fhould not be publifhed; and
fecondly, that they fhould not be lent out
of the library on any pretence whatever.

ever. A meeting of the College being
fummoned upon the occafion, Sir John's
donation was accepted with much gratitude; and a refolution paffed to comply
with the terms on which it was beftowed.
He was, at the fame time, preparing two
other volumes to be given to the Univerfity, containing the formulas referred to in
his annotations.

Sir John Pringle, upon his arrival at
the Metropolis, found his fpirits fomewhat
revived. He was greatly pleafed with
revifiting his London friends; and he was
received by them with equal cordiality and
affection. His Sunday evening conver-
fations were honoured with the attendance
of many refpectable men ; and, on the
other nights of the week, he had the
pleafure of fpending a couple of hours
with fuch friends as Lord Charles Cavendifh, Mr. Cavendifh, the Bifhop of Exe-

2   ter

ter (Dr. Rofs), Dr. Heberden, Dr. Watfon, Sir George Baker, Dr. Richard Saunders, Peter Holford Efquire, Ifrael Mau-
duit Efquire, and occafionally a few gentlemen befides. This was at a Society
that had long been eftablifhed, of which
Sir John Pringle had been many years a
Member; and which had met, for fome
time paft, at Mr. Watfon's, a grocer, in
the Strand. Sir John's connection with
this Society, and his conftant attendance
upon it, formed, to the laft, one of his
principal entertainments. The morning
was chiefly employed by him in receiving
and returning the vifits of his various
acquaintance; and he had frequently a fmall
and felect party to dine with him, at his
apartments in King's Street, St. James's
Square. All this while, his ftrength declined with a rapidity which did not permit
his friends to hope that his life would long
be continued. On Monday evening, the
fourteenth

fourteenth of January, 1782, being with
the fociety at Watfon's, he was feized with
a fit, from which he never recovered. He
was accompanied home by Dr. Saunders,
for whom he had the higheft regard, and
in whom he had, in every refpect, juftly
placed the moft unreferved confidence. The
Doctor afterwards attended him with unwearied affiduity, but, to any medical purpofe,
entirely in vain; for he departed this life on
the Friday following, being the eighteenth
day of the month, in the feventy-fifth year
of his age ; and the account of his death
was every where received, in a manner
which fhewed the high fenfe that was en-
tertained of his merit. On the feventh of
February, he was interred in St. James's
church, with great funeral folemnity, and
with a very honourable attendance of eminent and refpectable friends. As a teftimony of regard to his memory, at the firft
meeting of the College of Phyficians at

e   Edinburgh

Edinburgh after his deceafe, all the Members appeared in deep mourning.

Sir John Pringle, by long practice, had acquired a handfome fortune, which he difpofed of with great prudence and propriety. The bulk of it, as might naturally and reafonably be expected, he bequeathed to his worthy nephew and heir, Sir James Pringle, of Stichel, Bart. whom he appointed his fole executor. But the whole was not immediately to come to Sir James; for a fum equal, I believe, to feven hundred pounds a-year, was appropriated to annuities, revertible to that gentleman, at the deceafe of the annuitants. By this means, Sir John exhibited an important proof of his regard and affection for feveral of his valuable relations. He provided, likewife, for two fervants, who had lived with him a confiderable time ; and he left legacies to fome particular friends, among whom

whom the Writer of this Life had the honour of receiving a teſtimony of his remembrance and eſteem.

Sir John Pringle's eminent character as a
practical phyſician, as well as a medical
author, is ſo well known, and ſo univerſally acknowledged, that an enlargement
upon it cannot be neceſſary. He was dif-
tinguiſhed, in this reſpect, by his attention
and ſagacity. For the recovery of his pa-
tients he was anxiouſly concerned; and his
anxiety might, perhaps, be increaſed from
his conviction, that the art of Phyſic,
though eminently uſeful, muſt ever, from
unavoidable cauſes, be attended with a certain degree of uncertainty. His care was
rewarded with much ſucceſs in the courſe
of his practice. In the exerciſe of his
profeſſion, he was not rapacious; being
ready, on various occaſions, to give his
advice without pecuniary views. This he

never

never denied to the poor; and, from many
of his friends in better circumftances, and
who were well able to afford the cuftomary
gratifications, he refufed to accept of fees.

The turn of Sir John Pringle's mind led
him chiefly to the love of fcience, which he
built on the firm bafis of fact. With regard
to philofophy in general, he was as averfe
to theory, unfupported by experiments, as
he was with refpect to medicine in particular. Lord Bacon was his favourite author; and to the method of inveftigation,
recommended by that great man, he fteadily adhered. Such being his intellectual
character, it will not be thought furprifing,
that he had a diflike to Plato. The fpecu-
lations of that fublime and ingenious, that
elegant and beautiful, but at the fame time
fanciful writer, were by no means fuited to
the fober fpirit of enquiry cultivated by Sir

2   John

John Pringle. Indeed, whatever attention he might have paid, in his earlier days, and when he was Profeſſor of Ethics at Edinburgh, to metaphyſical diſquiſitions, he loſt all regard for them in the latter part of his life; and, though ſome of his moſt valued friends had engaged in diſcuſſions of this kind, with very different views of things*, he did not chooſe to revert to the ſtudies of his youth, but contented himſelf with the opinions he had then formed.

I ſhall not conceal from my readers, that Sir John Pringle had not much fondneſs for poetry †. He had not even any diſtin
· guiſhed

---

* Dr. Price, Dr. Prieſtley, and Lord Monboddo.

† That he was, however, himſelf the ſubject of poetical commendation, will appear from the following ſhort Latin Ode, which was addreſſed to him , in 1753, by Dr. Theobald:

Ode

guiſhed reliſh for the immortal Shakſpeare; at leaſt, he had too high a ſenſibility of the defects of that illuſtrious Bard, to give him the proper degree of eſtimation. The Writer of this account, who is one of the warmeſt admirers of our great Dramatiſt and Maſter of human nature, cannot men-

' Ode, Viro ingenio pariter ac docto, JOHANNI
' PRINGLE, M. D. et S. R. S. ſacra.

' DIVA Romana cata temperare
' Barbiton Cantu, O habilis modorum
' Artifex, feſtis mihi nuper horis
' Sæpe vocata!

' Fida PRINGELLI modulos coruſco
' Ede ſacratos merito, colendi
' Semper et culti, celebri revincti
' Tempore ſerto.

' Inclytis nulli viget is ſecundus
' Laudibus, tu ſive animum benignum
' Reſpicis, ſeu quo Medicum refulget
' Clarus honorem.

' Concini dignus meliore plectro,
' Fac, ut haud ſurda hoc bibat aure carmen,
' Conditum parva licet arte, grato at
' Pectore textum.'

(Nichols's Anecdotes of Bowyer, p. 601.)

tion

tion it in commendation of his Friend, that
he was defective in poetical tafte; but he
thinks it proper to be recorded, from a regard to truth, and to ftate a fact which
indicates the diverfity there is in the under-
ftandings, purfuits, and feelings of the
ableft men. The mind of Sir John Pringle was too clofely occupied by philofophical enquiries, to have much leifure or inclination for attending to the operations of
the imagination. Whether this be confidered as a defect in him or not, it was
certainly a lofs in point of real pleafure. A
relifh for poetry, and for thofe other compofitions by which the fancy is amufed,
affords a delightful relaxation, after more
fevere inveftigations. It tends to produce a
cheerfulnefs and hilarity of fpirits, which
may poffibly not a little contribute to health,
as well as to entertainment. Studies of this
nature not only *adolefcentiam alunt*, but

fenectutem

feuectutem oblectant. Nay, old age may derive a particular advantage from them, as they are calculated, by furnifhing agreeable and lively pictures to the imagination, to foothe the infirmities, and lighten the burdens, of that period.

Sir John Pringle had not, in his youth, been neglectful of philological enquiries; and, after having omitted them for a time, he returned to them again; fo far, at leaft, as to endeavour to obtain a more exact knowledge of the Greek tongue, probably with a view to a better underftanding of the New Teftament. He paid a great attention to the French language; and it is faid, that he was fond of Voltaire's critical writings. How far this might contribute to the honour of Sir John's tafte, I fhall not decide. However juft that eminent Frenchman's obfervations may have been on fome fubjects of criticifm, the truly

ingenious

ingenious and excellent Mrs. Montagu hath amply fhewn, that he was abfolutely unequal to the tafk of determining concerning the merit of Shakfpeare. Among all his other purfuits, Sir John Pringle never forgot the ftudy of the Englifh language. This he regarded as a matter of fo much confequence, that he took uncommon pains with refpect to the ftyle of his compofitions; and it cannot be denied, that he excels in perfpicuity, correctnefs, and propriety of expreffion.

Though our Author was not fond of Poetry, there was a fifter art for which he had a great affection, and that was Mufic. Of this art he was not merely an admirer, but became fo far a practitioner in it, as to be a performer on the violincello, at a weekly concert, given by a fociety of gentlemen at Edinburgh. Mufic, if not too eagerly purfued, or permitted to engrofs an

undue

undue proportion of time, is a fine relief to the mind of a literary man. It is often neglected, as perfons advance in years; and this, I believe, was the cafe with my Friend.

Befides a clofe application to medical and philofophical fcience, Sir John Pringle, during the latter part of his life, devoted much time to the ftudy of divinity. This was with him a very favourite and interefting object. He read many commentators on Scripture, and efpecially on the New Teftament, of which he was anxious to obtain an exact and critical knowledge. In this purfuit, the learned and judicious Bifhop Pearce's Commentary and Notes gave him particular pleafure, and were greatly fuited to his tafte. He correfponded frequently with Michaelis on theological fubjects; and that celebrated Profeffor addreffed to him fome letters on Daniel's

Prophecy

Prophecy of the Seventy Weeks, which Sir John thought worthy of being publiſhed in this country. Accordingly, he was at confiderable pains, and fome expence, in the publication, which appeared, in 1773, under the following title: ' Joannis Davi- ' dis Michaelis, Prof. Ordin. Philoſ. et Soc. ' Reg. Scient. Goettingenſis Collegæ, Epiſ- ' tolæ, de lxx Hebdomadibus Danielis, ad ' D. Joannem Pringle, Baronettum : pri- ' mò privatim miſſæ, nunc vero utriuſque ' conſenſu publicè editæ.' 8vo*.

Sir John Pringle was likewiſe a diligent and frequent reader of ſermons; which form a valuable part of Engliſh literature. Indeed, taken in their full extent, they conſtitute a much more valuable part of Engliſh literature, than, perhaps, is com- monly imagined. For, independently of

* Nichols's Biographical and Literary Anecdotes of William Bowyer, p. 446, 447. Ibid. p. 601.

their

their theological merit, in explaining the doctrines of Natural and Revealed Religion, and throwing light on paffages of Scripture, we fhall fcarcely any where meet with a richer treafure of practical obfervation, or with reflections on life and manners, that are better calculated to improve the underftanding, mend the heart, and regulate the conduct.

If, from the intellectual, we pafs on to the moral character of Sir John Pringle, we fhall find that the ruling feature of it was integrity. By this principle he was uniformly actuated in the whole of his behaviour. All his acquaintance will with one voice agree, that there never was an honefter man. He was equally diftinguifhed by his fobriety. He told Mr. James Bofwell, that he had never in his life been intoxicated with liquor; which muft be allowed to have been a very laudable

ble proof of the circumfpection maintained
by him, in the variety of company that he
had kept, both at home and abroad.

In his friendfhips, Sir John Pringle was
ardent and fteady. The intimacies which
were formed by him, in the early part of
his life, at Edinburgh, continued unbroken
to the deceafe of the gentlemen with whom
they were made; and were kept up by a
regular correfpondence, and by all the good
offices that lay in his power. One of his
oldeft and moft particular friends, was Mr.
Alexander Bofwell, afterwards Senator of
the College of Juftice, by the title of Lord
Auchinleck. Some unhappy differences
having taken place between Lord Auchinleck, and his fon Mr. James Bofwell, the
ingenious, worthy, and well-known author of the Account of Corfica, Sir John
Pringle was the benevolent and fuccefsful
mediator in procuring a reconciliation. In
allufion

allufion to this circumftance, he exprefled himfelf, in a letter to Mr. James Bofwell, written in 1773, in the following terms:
‘ I fhall be glad to ferve you. But remem-
‘ ber, in all cafes of oppofition, I fhall be
‘ on the minifterial fide; I mean, on that
‘ of your father, my oldeft and beft friend.
‘ You may inherit after him (if I fhould
‘ furvive him) my firft affections; but they
‘ cannot be alienated during his life.’

With relation to Sir John Pringle's external manner of deportment, he paid a very refpectful attention to thofe who were honoured with his friendfhip and efteem, and to fuch ftrangers as came to him well recommended. Foreigners, in particular, had great reafon to be fatisfied with the uncommon pains which he took to fhew them every mark of civility and regard. He had, however, at times, fomewhat of a drynefs and referve in his behaviour, which

had

had the appearance of coldnefs; and this was the cafe, when he was not perfectly pleafed with the perfons who were introduced to him, or who happened to be in his company. His fenfe of integrity and dignity would not permit him to adopt that falfe and fuperficial politenefs, which treats all men alike, though ever fo different in point of real eftimation and merit, with the fame fhew of cordiality and kindnefs. He was above affuming the profeffions, without the reality of refpect.

Dr. Johnfon hath thought it proper to be recorded of Pope, that, when he wanted to fleep, he ' nodded in company;' and that he once flumbered at his own table, while the Prince of Wales was talking of poetry. Sir John Pringle had this infirmity, efpecially in the latter part of his life. It chiefly appeared in the evening, and admits of a very eafy and juftifiable folution.

He

He had for many years been fo remarkably troubled for want of reft, that there was fcarcely a fingle night, in which he did not lie awake for feveral hours. He had this nocturnal wakefulnefs to a degree that rendered it a great affliction; and, therefore, it is not furprifing, that he fhould occafionally be overcome by drowfinefs. Neither can it be thought ftrange, that the fame caufe fhould have fome effect upon his fpirits. It was the principal, perhaps the fole reafon, of a certain wearifomenefs and reftleffnefs that hung about him, and which he fought to remove by changes of fituation.

On the religious character of Sir John Pringle it will be neceffary more particularly to enlarge; becaufe, fuch is the temper of the prefent age, that what is the greateft glory of any man, is often imputed to him as a weaknefs. The principles

ples of piety and virtue, which were early inftilled into our Author by a ftrict education, do not appear ever to have loft their influence upon the general conduct of his life. Neverthelefs, when he travelled abroad in the world, his belief of the Chriftian Revelation was fo far unfettled, that he became a fceptic with regard to it, if not a profeffed Deift. One caufe of this, was the wrong notions he had formed concerning the genuine doctrines of the New Teftament; and it will eafily be fuppofed, that he was encouraged in his fcruples by the company he met with both in England and in foreign parts. But it was not in the difpofition of Sir John Pringle, to reft fatisfied in his doubts and difficulties, with refpect to a matter of fuch high importance. He was too great a lover of truth, not to make Religion the object of his ferious enquiry. As he fcorned to be an implicit believer, he was equally averfe to

f   the

the being an implicit unbeliever; which is the cafe of large numbers, who reject Chriftianity with as little knowledge, and as little examination, as the moft determined bigots embrace the abfurdeft fyftem that ever was invented. The refult of his inveftigation was, a full conviction of the divine original and authority of the Gofpel. The evidence of Revelation appeared to him to be folid and invincible; and the nature of it to be fuch, as demanded his warmeft acceptance. What contributed entirely to remove the objections which had formerly lain upon his mind, was, his being perfectly fatisfied, that our holy religion did not contain fome doctrines which have commonly been thought to belong to it. There were three points that, in this view, appeared to him of great importance; and the removal of his difficulties, with regard to them, effaced every impreffion he might have received to the difadvantage of Chrift-ianity.

ianity. He became fully convinced, by
his ftudy of the Scriptures, that the Atha-
nafian doctrine of the Trinity made no part
of them; but that they uniformly con-
curred in afferting the unity and fupremacy
of the God and Father of Mankind. He
was equally convinced, that they did not
confine the mercy of the Supreme Being to
a few, exclufively of others; and that they
did not hold out any thing, with refpect to
the extent and duration of the future
punifhment of the wicked, which could in
the leaft be confidered as an impeachment
of the divine juftice, rectitude, and good-
nefs. In thefe fentiments, he agreed with
fome of the wifeft and beft men the world
hath ever produced, fome who have reflected the greateft honour on human nature. He was another inftance of thofe
illuftrious philofophers, who have not been
afhamed of religion; and added another
name to the catalogue of the excellent and

judicious

judicious perfons, who have gloried in being RATIONAL CHRISTIANS *.

As

* A late writer, whofe chief praife arifes from the
elegance and vivacity of his compofition, hath treated
the rational Chriftians with great contempt and feve-
rity, and, I·may add, with the higheft degree of injuftice. (Difquifitions on feveral Subjects, p. 101—
118.) He charges them with pretending to be
Chriftians, without believing; a charge which I have
no hefitation in aflerting to be abfolutely contrary to
truth. To accufe them, as he does, of want of fincerity, and to put them on a level with the Deifts,
can only proceed from the grofleft ignorance, or from
worfe motives; which I would not willingly impute
to any gentleman of character. There are none who
are more firmly perfuaded of the truth of the gofpel,
none who are more clearly convinced of its divine original, none who are more entirely fatisfied with the
weight and variety of its evidence, none who more
fincerely rejoice in its invaluable contents, than rational Chriftians. To men of this character the
world is indebted for the fulleft and ableft vindications
of the Old and New Teftament, againft the attacks
of Infidelity. From the men of this character have
proceeded thofe works in fupport of Natural and Revealed Religion, which will ftand the teft of ages, and
againft which the efforts of Scepticifm will be directed
in vain. Locke and Clarke, Hoadly and Sykes,
Butler and Jortin, Chandler and Fofter, Leland and

Lardner,

As Sir John Pringle was thus firmly perfuaded of the truth of the Gofpel, he lived
under

Lardner, Abernethy and Duchal, together with various other names that might be mentioned, were all
of them rational Chriftians. I prefume that few of
the able defenders of Revelation, which this country
has produced, would have chofen to be called irrational Chriftians. It is unfortunate for fuch an
irrational Chriftian as the Author of the Difquifitions,
that his mode of writing hath occafioned many perfons, who are ftrangers to his charaéter, to imagine
that he is an infidel in difguife, and that his defign
is to expofe our holy religion to contempt. For my
own part, I have no doubt of the fincerity of his
belief, and of the good intentions of his publications ;
but I think, at the fame time, that the manner in
which thefe intentions have been difplayed, is remarkably injudicious. With regard to rational Chriftians,
if there be fome doctrines, that have commonly been
received, to which they do not give their affent, this
doth not arife from the pride of human reafon, but
from their firm perfuafion, that fuch doctrines are not
to be found in the Scriptures. The Writer of the prefent Note can fincerely affert, that this is his own cafe.
Being entirely convinced of the truth of Revelation,
after a full, and, he trufts, a fair inveftigation of the
matter, the fole object of his enquiry is, What does
the Bible contain? what are the real dictates and de-
clarations of our Lord and his apoftles? Thofe

rational

under its influence. He was animated with a ftrong fenfe of piety to the Supreme Being,

rational Chriftians, who are fuppofed to depart the moft from the ftandards of faith generally eftablifhed, uniformly agree in maintaining a high fenfe of the invaluable bleffings derived from the Gofpel. They are fatisfied that thefe bleffings were beftowed in a fupernatural manner, by the God and Father of Mercies; that Jefus Chrift is the difpenfer of them; and that they confift of knowledge, pardon, purity, and everlafting happinefs. They believe that eternal life is not only revealed by our Saviour, but abfolutely afcertained by his death and refurrection. This is a point, the importance of which no words can exprefs. With what juftice, then, can any one degrade into the rank of Deifts, the men who are fully perfuaded, that ' the gift of God is eternal life, through Jefus Chrift ' our Lord ?' Every man, who knows the world, muft be fenfible, that the far greater part of thofe who difcard Revealed Religion, have little or no expectation of a future ftate. But there is not a fingle perfon, among fuch as are called Rational Chriftians, who will not fay, with the warmeft gratitude, ' This ' is the record, that God hath given to us eternal life, ' and this life is in his Son.'

It is an obfervation of great moment, and which, therefore, deferves to be attended to, that the believers in Chriftianity do not differ fo much in their fentiments

Being, which difplayed itfelf in a regular
attendance upon public worfhip, in the

ments concerning the nature and value of the bleffings
derived from the Gofpel, as with refpect to fome
other queftions. They are all agreed, that, when
mankind were ignorant and guilty, corrupt, and liable
to a fentence of eternal death, the Saviour appeared, to
communicate fpiritual inftruction, to beftow upon
them the forgivenefs of fin, to purify their hearts and
regulate their conduct, and to raife them up to everlafting felicity and glory. Of the unfpeakable excellence, and immenfe greatnefs, of thefe benefits,
Chriftians are alike fenfible, and alike afcribe them to
the Revelation of Jefus, however they may vary in
their opinions concerning the caufes, or the effects of
the caufes, which brought men into their wretched
condition; and whatever ideas they may have formed
concerning the dignity of the Perfon by whom the
bleffings of the Gofpel are conveyed, and the peculiar
operation of his fufferings. Were it, therefore, ever
fo certain, that the rational Chriftians are miftaken in
their fentiments, the charge brought againft them by
the Writer of the Difquifitions, would ftill be equally
uncandid and ill-founded. He is not the only Author
who has preferred againft them the fame accufation.
Others have reprefented them as being no better than
Deifts: but fuch manifeft ignorance, bigotry, and
injuftice, ought long ago to have been banifhed from
this kingdom.

exercife

exercife of private devotion, and in an endeavour to difcharge all the obligations of
virtue. Such being the tenour of his life
and conduct, and deriving great confola-
tion from Chriftianity, as an inftitution of
mercy, he rejoiced in a fenfe of the Divine
favour, and in the hope of future happinefs. Neverthelefs, whether from a confti-
tutional timidity of temper, or from early
impreffions, or from the ftate of his body,
the approaches of death were met by him
with fome degree of apprehenfion. This
was not an apprehenfion with regard to its
confequences, but a certain kind of awful-
nefs with relation to the thing itfelf; a difpofition which has been experienced by
many worthy perfons. The wakefulnefs
before mentioned, with which our Author
was afflicted for fo many years, will, perhaps, fatisfactorily account for this failure
of fpirits; and to the fame caufe it may be
afcribed, if, in any other refpect, he did

not

not fuftain the infirmities of age with that full fortitude and dignity of mind, which, though always defirable, cannot, even by the beft characters, always be attained.

Sir John Pringle's literary and other connections were fo very numerous, that only a fmall part of them can here be fpecified. Several of his learned and philofophical acquaintance have already been occafionally mentioned; and if, in adding a few more names to the lift, I fhould be guilty of any improper omiffions, it will, I hope, be imputed to what alone it is owing, either to a want of information or recollection, or to the difficulty of choice, amidft fuch a variety of objects. In early life, our Author entered into a clofe friendfhip with the moft diftinguifhed perfons of the city of Edinburgh; and with fome

of

of them he maintained a regular correfpondence *. The eminent philofopher,
Maclaurin, was his intimate friend; of
whofe memory he expreffes himfelf, in one
of his Difcourfes, with peculiar affection,
and whom he always fpoke of, in converfation, with the higheft marks 'of efteem
and regard. When he returned to Edinburgh, with the purpofe of ending his days
in that city, there were ftill living, of his
old acquaintance, Dr. George Wifhart, Sir
Alexander Dick, Dr. Hope, Dr. Steddman,

---

* Sir Alexander Dick has preferved a feries of letters from Sir John Pringle, being forty-feven in
number. They difplay the excellence of his character in a full light, and fhew the warmth and fteadinefs
of his friendfhip. They contain, likewife, many
valuable articles in Medicine and Natural Philofophy,
accurately and pleafingly expreffed. His letters to
Lord Auchinleck (whom he calls his firft and beft of
friends), to Mr. James Bofwell, to Dr. Steddman,
and other gentlemen, exhibit him in the fame advantageous point of view.

and,

and, perhaps, fome others, of whom I have not been particularly informed. The lofs he had fuftained, in the deceafe of feveral of his former companions, was in part made up by their fons; among whom Mr. Bofwell, Mr. Wallace, Mr. Murray (then Solicitor General for Scotland, and now one of the Lords of Seffion), and Mr. Maclaurin, diftinguifhed themfelves in difplaying every proof of attachment and refpect to the man, who had been the intimate friend of each of their fathers.

Of Sir John Pringle's acquaintance in England, it would not be eafy to give a detail. Were I to attempt fuch a detail, it would include a large number of the moft worthy and eminent characters, of all profeffions. His converfation was not confined to medical gentlemen, though his

intercourfe

intercourfe with them was very great, but extended to many perfons of rank and confequence, as well as merit. He liked much to converfe with the liberal-minded clergy, whether of the eftablifhment, or among the Diffenters; and he was honoured with the friendfhip and efteem of fome of the moft excellent and learned prelates of the church. Among the diftinguifhed philofophers of the age, there were few with whom he was not clofely connected; and he had a particular intimacy with Dr. Franklin, till it was interrupted by the unfortunate public contefts, which carried that celebrated man to another country, and another fcene of action.

Without pretending diftinctly to fpecify Sir John Pringle's more private friends, who were numerous and highly refpectable, I muft be permitted to mention Edward Mafon

Mafon Efq. (formerly Secretary to his Royal Highnefs William Duke of Cumberland), with whom our Author formed an acquaintance in Germany; which continued, with unbroken efteem and affection, to the end of life. To this gentleman he bequeathed a teftimony of remembrance in his laft will. For feveral years before his deceafe, there was no one in whom he placed fo unreferved a confidence, and for whom he had ftronger regard, than Dr. Richard Saunders. His fenfe of the Doctor's zealous attention and friendfhip was particularly expreffed, by leaving to him his prints and drawings.

It would be impoffible for me to do full juftice to Sir John Pringle's connections with foreigners. There were no perfons who vifited England, if they had any tafte for philofophical fcience, that were not recommended

cômmended to him, and did not cultivate
his acquaintance. Befides this, he correfponded with many eminent philofophers
and phyficians, whom he had never feen.
Whether he ever had an opportunity of
being perfonally acquainted with Linnæus,
Baron Van Haller, and Tiffot, I do not
recollect; but he maintained an epiftolary
intercourfe with them, and with almoft
every diftinguifhed name in Europe, and
efpecially in Germany, France, and Hol-
land. How far, and to whom, his correfpondence extended, might have been more
exactly fpecified, if he had not burnt all his
letters before his deceafe. The celebrated
Abbé Fontana, during the time of his being in England, was much in the company
of Sir John Pringle: but there was no
foreigner who, at the different periods of
his refidence in this country, enjoyed fo
great an intimacy with him as Dr. Ingen-
houfz.

houfz. This gentleman was recommended by Sir John to the Emprefs Queen of, Hungary, and to the Emperor of Germany, as a proper perfon to inoculate the Imperial and Auftrian family ; in the fuccefsful per- formance of which, he attained to diftin- guifhed emoluments and honours. The high fenfe which he had of his obligations to our Author, in this and in other refpects, he has expreffed in a very handfome dedi- cation, prefixed to his curious ' Experi- ' ments upon Vegetables.' This was not the only book dedicated to Sir John Prin- gle. We have already feen, that Michaelis paid him a fimilar teftimony of regard ; and the fame was done by Baron Van Haller, in one of his publications. The reputation in which our Author was held abroad, was uncommonly great ; and was productive of every mark of attention and efteem.

Such

Such having been the character and eminence of Sir John Pringle, it was highly proper that his name fhould be recorded among the Worthies of Weft-minfter Abbey. Accordingly, under the direction, and at the expence, of his Nephew and Heir, a monument is preparing, of which Mr. Nollekens is the fculptor, and for which an Englifh infcription is intended.

If it had been determined to have had a Latin infcription, there was one, written by a gentleman of the firft claffical knowledge and tafte, which would undoubtedly have had the preference. I have obtained leave to infert it ; and it gives me pleafure that I can conclude my account of Sir John Pringle with fo elegant and honourable a teftimony to his memory.

M. S.

M. S.

Viri egregii JOHANNIS PRINGLE Baronetti;
Quem exercitus Britannicus,
Celfiffima Walliæ Principeffa,
Regina fereniffima,
Ipfius denique Regis Majeftas,
Medicum fibi comprobavit
Experientiffimum, fagacem, ftrenuum:
Quem, ftudiis academicis florentem,
Edinburgenfes olim fui
In cathedrâ difciplinæ ethicæ dicatâ
Adhuc juvenem collocârunt:
Quem pofteà, ætate ac fcientiâ provectum,
Primùm perhonorifico ornavit prœmio,
Deindè ad fummam apud fe dignitatem evexit
Societas Regia Londinenfis.
Qualis fuerit medendi artifex,
Quali rerum comprehenfione præditus,
Materiem fuam multiplicem
Quam fcientèr explicuerit et illuftraverit,
Scripta Viri doctiffimi teftentur
Per Europam omnem diffeminata,
Nec forìs minùs quam domi nota.
Quâ autem fide et integritate fuerit,
Quam veri tenax et inimicus fraudi,
Quam conftans Supremi Numinis cultor,
Ii, quibufcum vixit,
Teftes funto.

Exceffit e vitâ, &c.

g

SIX

DISCOURSES,

DELIVERED BY

Sir JOHN PRINGLE, Bart.

BEFORE THE

ROYAL SOCIETY;

On occasion of Six Annual Assignments of

SIR GODFREY COPLEY's MEDAL.

g 2

A

DISCOURSE

ON THE

DIFFERENT KINDS OF AIR,

DELIVERED AT THE

Anniverſary Meeting of the ROYAL SOCIETY,
November 30, 1773.

By Sir JOHN PRINGLE, Bart. PRESIDENT,

PUBLISHED AT THEIR REQUEST.

B

A

DISCOURSE

ON THE

DIFFERENT KINDS OF AIR.

GENTLEMEN,

IT is with great fatisfaction I enter upon this part of my office—to confer, in your name, the prize-medal of the prefent year upon a Member of this Society fo worthy of that diftinction.

THE object which Sir GODFREY COP-LEY, founder of the benefaction, had in

view,

view, and the manner in which the original pecuniary reward was converted into
this more liberal form, having been ſo
lately explained by my honoured predeceſ-
ſor; I need only obſerve, that though your
Preſident and Council have been entruſted
with the ſole power of adjudging this premium, yet they have now, as, I am per-
ſuaded, they have had on former occaſions,
the greateſt ſolicitude to nominate that
perſon, who, in their opinion, would have
obtained all your ſuffrages.

In confidence of ſuch unanimity, it is
with ſingular pleaſure I acquaint you, that
the Reverend JOSEPH PRIESTLEY, Doctor
of Laws, has been found at this time the
beſt entitled to ſo public a mark of your
approbation, on account of the many curious and uſeful experiments contained in
his *Obſervations on different Kinds of Air*,
read at the Society in March 1772, and
inſerted

inferted in the laft complete volume of
your Tranfactions *. And indeed, GEN-
TLEMEN, when you refleet on the zeal
which our worthy brother has fhewn to
ferve the Public, and to do credit to your
Inftitution, by his numerous, learned, and
valuable communications, you will, I imagine, be inclined to think, that we have
been rather flow than precipitate in acknowledging fo much merit.

YOUR time will not allow me to touch on
the fubjects of his former Papers † : nay, I
apprehend I fhall even trefpafs upon it, by
recalling to your memory only a few of
thofe interefting difcoveries which Doctor
PRIESTLEY has made in thefe *Obfervations:*
fince, in doing juftice to others as well as
to him, it will be proper to remind you of
the progrefs that had already been made in

* Vol. lxii.
† In Phil. Tranf. vol. lviii, lix, lx.

B 3   this

this part of fcience by men of the greateft abilities in their time, and by other ingenious perfons ftill among us.

THERE is not perhaps any branch of Natural philofophy that has more engaged the attention of the learned, or been more fuccefsfully cultivated, than the nature of the common air. The knowledge how indifpenfable it is to the prefervation of animals, muft have been coëval with mankind : it was from the beginning, as now, *the breath of life.* It was found likewife to be a neceffary fupport of fire, and they faw that the vegetable creation, deprived of it, languifhed and died. Nor did the ancient phyficians fail to diftinguifh, at leaft attempt to diftinguifh, between the effects of an air too hot and one too cold, an air too moift and one too dry, and between an infalutary and a wholefome air.—Thus far the experience, or the theory of all ages.—

4   But

But the lefs obvious properties of this element, its gravitation and its elafticity, with
their long train of confequences, remained
unknown, till, about the beginning of the laft
century, Lord BACON and GALILEO, in
that dawn of philofophy which they themfelves diffufed, began the inquiry. The
former, from experiments, afcertained the
elafticity of the air ; and upon that principle conftructed his *vitrum calendare*, the
firft thermometer *. The latter difcovered
that air had weight ; but though that ornament of Italy was not ignorant of the
limited fuction of a pump, yet to account
for the rife of the water fo far in it, he ftill
had recourfe to Nature's *abhorrence of a
void* †.

TORRICELLI, at laft, the difciple of
GALILEO, by one happy and decifive ex-

* Bac. Nov. Org. lib. ii. aph. 13.
† Dialog. i.

B 4   periment,

periment, difcovered the preffure of the
atmofphere; and PASCAL obferved, that
this preffure varied according to the heights
he carried his barometer *. Soon after followed the air-pump, the invention of the
celebrated OTTO DE GUERICK; which,
though at firft a rude and imperfect inftrument, yet, improved by himfelf †, and
more by Mr. BOYLE and Dr. HOOK (two
of the illuftrious fathers of this fociety), it
foon became, in the hands of Mr. BOYLE,
the means of opening the richeft mines of
natural knowledge. In this refearch, the
Hiftory of the Common Air, he feemed fo
far to carry his inquiries, as to leave little
to be done by others who fhould come after
him; thofe parts excepted, depending on
geometry and calculation ‡. How fuccefs-

* Traité fur l'Equilibre des Liq.

† Gafpar. Schott. De Arte Mechan. Hydr. Pneu-
mat. Exp. nova Magdeburgh.

‡ Boyle, Phyfico-mechan. Exp. & Mem. for a
Gen. Hift. of the Air.

fully

fully thefe were executed by Dr. HALLEY
and Sir ISAAC NEWTON, I fcarcely need
to mention ; nor the folid foundation on
which thofe great men eftablifhed the rare-
faction of the air ; and in what proportion,
according to its diftance from the earth *.
But it was Sir ISAAC NEWTON alone,
who, upon the principle of the air's being
compreffed by the power of gravity, and
that of its elafticity, taught that tremulous
bodies would communicate their motion to
the air, and thereby excite vibrations in it,
fpreading every where. Thus he difcovered
the efficient caufe of founds †.

BUT, before this period, Mr. BOYLE
obferving, as he himfelf informs us, how
much air was concerned in many of the
phænomena of Nature, and how neceffary

* Phil. Tranf. No. 181. p. 104. Abrid. vol. ii.
p. 14. Phil. Nat. Princ. Math. lib. ii. prop. 22, 23.
† Phil. Nat. Princ. Mat. lib. ii. prop. 43.

it was to the exiftence of animals, became
folicitous to inquire, whether a fluid of fo
great importance were not producible by
art; if fo, he believed that fuch air might
be ferviceable in life, particularly in the art
of diving, and in *fubmarine navigation* *.
With thefe views that admirable Naturalift
fet about making fome new experiments,
and, from a variety of bodies, by different
proceffes, obtained a pneumatical fluid
(from ripe fruit, fermenting and effervefcing
liquors, and from the putrefaction of animal and vegetable fubftances) anfwering,
till then, his only criterion of air, in being
of a durably elaftic nature †. Yet after all,
Mr. BOYLE found that thefe new productions were effentially different from common air, as they prefently extinguifhed
flame, and fuffocated thofe animals that

* An attempt of Cornelius Drebell to make a veffel
to row under water with men in it. See Boyle's Works,
vol. i. p. 69; vol. iii. p. 174.

† Boyle's Works, vol. iv. p. 236, & feq.

attempted

attempted to breathe in them. But though he miffed finding what he fo much wanted, his labour was not in vain : philofophy was enriched with the knowledge of what he called *fa&itious* or *artificial* air, which has in the end proved as ufeful as he could have wifhed, in explaining feveral natural appearances, and in being fubfervient to the wants of man.

But this difcovery, however interefting to the Naturalift, and to the Chemift in particular *, feems to have been little attended to, till, in the beginning of this century, Sir Isaac Newton obferved, that true permanent air arifes from fixed bodies by heat and fermentation ; and that thofe aërial particles recede from one another with the greateft force, which upon contaᵭt cohered moft ftrongly :—and that denfe bodies by fermentation rarefy into

* Hales, Stat. Eff. vol. i. ch. 6. p. 317.

feveral

feveral forts of air; and that this air, by
fermentation, and fometimes without it,
returns into denfe bodies *. Excited by
fuch authority, the Reverend Dr. HALES
(whofe amiable as well as philofophic qualities are ftill frefh on the minds of feveral
gentlemen prefent), refuming thofe experiments concerning the feparation of air from
bodies, confirmed and extended the difcoveries of Mr. BOYLE; fhewing not only
that air entered into the compofition of
moft bodies, but the very proportion it bore
to the reft of the compound, and that often
to an amazing quantity †. Dr. HALES
likewife examined the mineral waters, thofe
of Pyrmont particularly; and, finding them
abounding with air, to that circumftance
he afcribed the fpirit and brifknefs of thofe
fountains. But that excellent author did
not feem to apprehend, that in this, as in

* Compare Newton's Optics, Quer. 30, 31.
† Stat. Eff. vol. i. ch. 6.

other

other inftances, the air which he produced
was not the common air, but, if I may be
allowed the expreffion, the *factitious* air of
Nature; as being of the fame kind with
what Mr. BOYLE had extracted from fermenting and effervefcing liquors; nay, the
fame with the *mephitis* or deadly vapour of
the ancients, or the *mofeta* of the modern
Italians, fo frequently met with in the ca-
verns, fprings, and lakes of their country:
and the fame with the *ftith* or *choak-damp*
in our coal-pits, fo often fatal to the
miners. It muft be owned it was hard to
conceive, how thefe fprings fhould owe
their prime virtues to what, in another
manner of application, Dr. HALES faw was
fo deftructive of vitality.

Now this notion, concerning the im-
pregnation of the mineral waters by the
mephitis, was, as far as I know, originally
fuggefted by a foreign Member, Dr. SEIP of
Pyrmont,

Pyrmont, firſt in a treatiſe he publiſhed in the German language, and afterwards in a communication to this Society, in the year 1736, in which he deſcribes a ſmall cavern at Pyrmont, ſimilar to the *grotta de' cani*, near Naples *. But when this ingenious author calls that *mephitis* (which is a durably elaſtic fluid *ſui generis*) a *ſulphureous ſteam*, or a *ſulphureo-ſpirituous vapour*, he appears to have been imperfectly acquainted with its nature; which is now found to conſiſt of nothing inflammable or ſulphureous, and to be of a denſity, or ſpecific gravity, conſiderably greater than that of common air.

THE fuller diſcovery of this prin-ciple we owe to Dr. BROWNRIGG of Whitehaven, who, about thirty years ago, began clearly to unfold this myſtery. But his curious papers were not then inſerted

* Phil. Tranſ. No. 448. Abridg. vol. viii. p. 659.

in

in the Tranfactions, as the too modeft Author had requefted a delay, till he fhould
be able to make them more worthy of that
honour. In his communication he remarks, ' That a more intimate acquaint-
' ance with thofe noxious airs in mines,
' called *damps*, might lead to the difcovery
' of that fubtile principle of mineral waters,
' known by the name of their *fpirit*; that
' the mephitic exhalations, termed the
' *choak-damp*, he had found to be a fluid
' permanently elaftic; and from various
' experiments he had reafon to conclude,
' that it entered the compofition of the
' waters of Pyrmont, Spa, and others;
' imparting to them that pungent tafte,
' from which they were denominated *aci-
' dulæ*, and likewife that volatile principle,
' on which their virtues chiefly depend *.'

In order to afcertain a fact of fo much
confequence, Dr. BROWNRIGG took the

* Vid. Phil. Tranf. vol. lv. p. 236. & feq.

opportunity,

opportunity, when at Spa feveral years after, to make fome experiments for this purpofe ; when he had the fatisfaction to find thofe waters pregnant with the *arti-ficial* or *factitious* air of Mr. BOYLE, the fame with that of the fuffocating *grotta* near Naples, and the fame with the *choak-damp* of our coal-mines ; forafmuch as this air inftantly extinguifhed flame, and the life of thofe animals he had inclofed in it*. The fuccefs of this worthy Member, in thus far analyzing thofe waters, encouraged others to purfue the inquiry ; and to in-veftigate the manner in which Nature alfo furnifhed them with the chalybeate prin-ciple †. Mr. LANE therefore, in confe-quence of a converfation with Dr. WAT-SON junior (both of this Society), upon an experiment of Mr. CAVENDISH's, by which that gentleman had found the me-

---

* Vid. Phil. Tranf. vol. lv. p. 218. & feq,
† More properly, the *iron-principle*.

phitic

phitic air (fuch as Dr. BROWNRIGG had detected in Spa-water) fufficient to diffolve any calcarious earth *: in confequence, I fay, of this converfation, wherein it was furmifed, that the fame mephitic air might likewife diffolve iron in common water, Mr. LANE made the experiment with air taken from Spa water, and happily fuc-ceeded †. By this means the nature of the metallic principle, in mineral waters, was clearly explained ; and the whole analyfis of thofe celebrated fountains, fo often attempted by chemifts and others, and ftill eluding their laboured refearches, was thus, in the moft fimple manner, brought to light.

NOTHING now feemed to be wanting to the triumph of Art, but an eafy manner of joining, as there fhould be occafion, one or

---

* Phil. Tranf. vol. lvii. p. 92. & feq.
† Ib. vol. lix. p. 216. & feq.

both

both of thefe principles to common water,
in order to improve upon Nature, in the
more extenfive ufe of her medicine. This
was effected by Dr. PRIESTLEY, after fome
other important difcoveries had been made
in this part of Pneumatics, firft by Dr.
BLACK, Profeffor of Chemiftry at Edinburgh, and then by Mr. CAVENDISH of
this Society. The former has fhewn that a
particular fpecies of factitious air (he calls
it *fixed*) adheres to all calcarious earths,
magnefia, and alcaline falts, with different
degrees of force ; and that this fluid can be
feparated from thefe fubftances, and combined again with them, in the fame manner as an acid. Upon this difcovery he
explained in a clear and fimple manner
many appearances in chemiftry, till then
deemed the moft unaccountable. Such was
the effervefcence of abforbent earths and
alkaline falts with acids, and the change of
the mild calcarious earths into quick lime

by

by heat (in confcquence of the expulfion of this *fixed* air which neutralizes them) *. I muft add, that I have been well informed, that, for feveral years paft, the learned Profeffor has taught, that the air which unites with alkaline fubftances is of the fame nature with the *mephitis*, or fuffocating air of the *grotta de' cani* and mines; the fame with what is emitted from vegetables in fermentation; and that in fome refpeas it agrees with the air which has been injured by the breath of animals, or by the burning of fuel: and laftly, that the air or elaftic fluid arifing from the folution of mctals by acids is very different from the former.

MR. CAVENDISH has made feveral valuable additions to thefe difcoveries, not only with regard to that fpecies of *faclitious* air the Profeffor had denominated *fixed air*,

* Eff. and Obferv. Phyf. & Liter. vol. ii, p. 157. & feq.

but

but to other elaftic fluids. He has with
accuracy afcertained the fpecific gravity of
this fixed air, as expelled from alkaline
fubftances by acids, or from vegetable
matter by fermentation ; and has demonftrated the fimilarity of airs produced by
either of thefe two ways. He has confirmed Dr. BLACK's account of the quantity of the fixed air contained in alkaline falts
and in alkaline earths. He has fhewn that
this fluid can be mixed with water, and in
what proportion ; and that it flies off again
from the water, upon heating it, or ex-
pofing it to the common air. Laftly, that
this fpecies of factitious air imparts to the
water the power of diffolving abforbent
earths ; the experiment, as I obferved before, which led to the knowledge, how
Nature infufed the metallic principle into
what are commonly called the *chalybeate*
waters *.

* Phil. Tranf. vol. lvi. p. 141. & feq.

OF

OF all thefe facts Dr. PRIESTLEY has carefully availed himfelf. For having learned from Dr. BLACK that this fixed or mephitic air could in great abundance be procured from chalk, by means of diluted fpirit of vitriol *; from Dr. MACBRIDE, that this fluid was of a confiderable antifeptic nature †; from Mr. CAVENDISH, that it could, in a large quantity, be abforbed by water ‡; and from Dr. BROWN-RIGG, that it was this very air which gave the brifknefs and chief virtues to the Spa and Pyrmont waters §: Dr. PRIESTLEY, I fay, fo well inftructed, conceived that common water, impregnated with this fluid alone, might be ufeful in medicine, particularly for failors on long voyages, for curing or preventing the fea-fcurvy. This,

* Eff. and Obferv. Phyf. & Liter. loc. cit.
† Experim. Eff. paffim.
‡ Phil. Tranf. vol. lvi. p. 161. & feq.
§ Phil. Tranf. vol. lv. p. 218. & feq.

we

we know, is a putrid diftemper, requiring
all the antifeptic quality of thofe mineral
waters, without the chalybeate principle,
which might injure, by over-heating the
blood, too much difpofed to inflammation.
For this purpofe, he made a fimple apparatus, for generating this fpecies of air from
chalk, and mixing it with water, in fuch
quantities, and in fo fpeedy a manner,
that, having exhibited the experiment before this Society, and the College of Phyficians, it met with fo much approbation,
that, in order the Public might the focner
reap the benefit of it, he was induced to
detach this part of his labours, and in a
feparate Paper to prefent it to the Admiralty *.

THE reft of his obfervations upon the
different kinds of air, addreffed to the So-

* A pamphlet intitled, Directions for impregnating
Water, &c.

7   ciety,

ciety *, contain fo much matter, that I
will not prefume to encroach fo far on your
time, as to offer even a fhort abftract of the
whole ; but fhall be fatisfied to fingle out a
few of thofe many difcoveries, fuch as are
the moft ftriking, either for their immediate
ufe in life, like that above ; or for the ex-
planation of fome of the more interefting
appearances in Nature.

I come, therefore, to another fpecies of
factitious air, called the *inflammable*. Till
within thefe few years, little more was
known, than that this kind of fubtile fluid
was found in mines, in neglected privies,
and common fewers ; but chiefly in coal-
pits, where it is called the *fire-damp*, making fometimes formidable explofions, and
indeed often fatal to the miners. I do not
recollect that Mr. Boyle has taken any
other notice of it †. But, about forty years

* Phil. Tranf. vol. lxii.
† Boyle's Works, vol. iii. p. 101.; vol. v. p. 305,
306.

ago,

ago, Sir JAMES LOWTHER, Baronet, favoured the Society with an account, fomewhat more particular, of this production of
his coal-mines in Cumberland, accompanying it with feveral bladders filled with
that fluid, which, in this houfe, burnt as
readily, as at its fource a month before.
Yet ftill this extraordinary fubftance was
confidered more as an object of curiofity,
than as one of philofophical inquiry, till
Mr. CAVENDISH began to make experiments upon it; by which, and the confequences drawn from them, he has added
another confiderable branch to the doctrine
of aërial fluids.

FIRST, he has taught how to produce at
will, and in great abundance, this other
permanently elaftic fluid from three metallic bodies, Zinc, Iron, and Tin, by diffolving them in the diluted vitriolic acid, or
fpirit of fea-falt. This fpecies of factitious
air he has fhewn to be furprizingly light,
being

being no more than the tenth part of the
weight of common air, and therefore totally different from the *mephitis*, that other
fpecies of factitious air we have been treating of, and which, as 'was obferved, is
heavier than the air of our atmofphere.
Laftly, Mr. CAVENDISH has given feveral
experiments upon the inflammability of
various mixtures of this fluid with common
air, which are likewife new ; and, like
the reft, have been made with great pre-
cifion.

Now, though Dr. PRIESTLEY has alfo
improved upon this enquiry, by the addition of a variety of experiments ; in particular, by fhewing how this air becomes
mifcible with water, and deprived of its
inflammability ; by comparing it with other
fpecies of factitious air, in regard to con-
ducting the electrical fluid ; by enquiring
how far it may be confidered as common

air,

air, loaded with the principle of fire, called *phlogiſton* by the modern chemiſts; with other curious obſervations on this ſubſtance: yet all theſe, with other kinds of faɑitious air, as I have already too long detained you, I muſt with regret paſs over; one other ſpecies excepted, as I reckon it among the moſt brilliant of Dr. PRIESTLEY's diſcoveries *.

THIS ſpecies he calls the *nitrous air*, without infiſting on the propriety of the expreſſion. It was firſt produced from the Walton pyrites, by means of the ſpirit of nitre. Dr. HALES, who made the experi-

---

* I might have added another new ſpecies of faɑitious air, which he terms *acid*, firſt taken notice of by Mr. CAVENDISH, and more fully inveſtigated by Dr. PRIESTLEY. This is an elaſtic vapour, expelled by heat from ſpirit of ſalt, and not liable afterwards to be condenſed by cold. Water readily imbibes this air, and by that means becomes a ſtrong ſpirit of ſalt. The ſame acid air, or vapour, he has alſo diſcovered to be a decompoſer of ſubſtances that contain *phlogiſton*, and with them to form a proper inflammable air.

ment,

ment, obferved that, when joined to common air, an effervefcence enfued, with a turbid red colour of the mixture, and an abforption of part of the common air *. Dr. PRIESTLEY, extending the experiment to other metallic fubftances, obferved, that the fame kind of air was by the fame acid readily procured from iron, copper, brafs, tin, filver, quickfilver, bifmuth, and nickel; and that though it conftantly, when joined to common air, exhibited thofe appearances mentioned by Dr. HALES, and more confpicuoufly in proportion to the purity of the common air mixed with it (that is, its fitnefs for refpiration); yet it made no change with either fixed or inflammable air, or that air tainted by the breath of animals, or the corruption of their bodies. By means of this teft, he was enabled to judge of the kind, as well

* Stat. Eff. vol. ii. p. 280.

as of the degree of injury, done to common
air, by candles burning in it; and to perceive a real difference in the air of his
ſtudy, after a few perſons had been with
him there. Nay, a phial of air having
been ſent him from the neighbourhood of
a large town, it appeared, upon a compa-
rative trial, to be inferior in quality to that
taken up near Leeds, where he then re-
ſided. It was upon ſuch a proſpect of obtaining a criterion for diſtinguiſhing good
air from bad, that Lord BACON almoſt in
a rapture breaks out: ' Theſe are noble
' experiments, that can make this diſco-
' very; for they ſerve for a natural divina-
' tion of ſeaſons !' and again, ' They teach
' men to chuſe their dwelling for their bet-
' ter health *.'

Nor is this all the uſe of the nitrous air:
Dr. PRIESTLEY ſhews it to be one of the

* Nat. Hiſt. Exp. 777.

ſtrongeſt

ftrongeft antifeptics. The fixed air has
been proved by Dr. MACBRIDE, as was
remarked, to be powerful in this particular ; but this fpecies of factitious air has
been found to be of fuperior efficacy. And
as our Author has difcovered it to be mifcible with water, he has reafon to believe
it may be applied to various purpofes, fuch
as the prefervation of the more delicate
birds, fiſhes, fruits, and anatomical preparations.

I SHALL now conclude with fhewing
from Dr. PRIESTLEY, what refources Nature has in ftore againſt the bad effects of
corrupted air, which from various caufes
infect our atmofphere.

IT is well known that flame cannot long
fubfift without a renewal of common air.
The quantity of that fluid, which even a
fmall flame requires, is furprifing : an ordinary

nary candle *confumes*, as it is called, about a gallon of air in a minute. Now, confidering the vaft confumption of this vital fluid by fires of all kinds made by man, and by volcanos, it becomes an interefting enquiry, to afcertain what change is made in the air by flame; and to difcover what provifion there is in Nature, to repair the injury done by this means to our atmofphere. Dr. PRIESTLEY, after relating the conjectures of others, and not finding them fatisfactory, was fortunate in falling upon a method of reftoring air, which had been vitiated by the burning of candles in it. This led the way to the difcovery of one of the great reftoratives which Nature employs for this purpofe, to wit, vegetation. See by what induction he proves his opinion.

IT was natural to imagine, that, fince the change of common air is neceffary to vegetable, as well as to animal life, both

plants

plants and animals rendered it foul in the fame manner, fo as to become unfit for farther life and vegetation. But when with that expectation the Doctor had put a fprig of mint, in a growing and vigorous ftate, under an inverted glafs jar ftanding in water, he was agreeably difappointed to find, that this plant not only continued to live, though in a languifhing way, for two months, but that the confined air was fo little corrupted by what had iffued from the mint, that it would neither extinguifh a candle, nor kill a fmall animal which he conveyed into it. What farther evinced the falutary nature of the *effluvia* of vegetables; he found that air, vitiated by a candle left in it till it burnt out, was perfectly reftored to its quality of fupporting flame, after another fprig of mint had for fome time vegetated in it. And to fhew that the aromatic vapour of that plant had no fhare in reftoring this purity to the air, he

he obferved, that vegetables of an offenfive
fmell, and even fuch as fcarcely had any
fmell at all, but were of a quick growth,
proved the very beft for this purpofe. Nay
more, the virtue of growing vegetables was
found to be an antidote to the baneful quality of air corrupted by animal refpiration
and putrefaction.

WE have faid, that neither candles will
burn, nor animals live, beyond a certain
time in a given quantity of air; yet the
caufe of either fo fpeedy a death or extinc-
tion was unknown; nor was any method
difcovered for rendering that empoifoned
air fit again for refpiration. Some provifion however there muft be in Nature for
this purpofe, as well as for that of fupporting flame: without fuch, the whole atmofphere would in time become unfit for animal life, and the race of men, as well as
beafts, would die of a peftilential diftemper.

Yet

Yet we have reafon to believe, that in our day the air is not lefs proper for breathing in, than it was above two thoufand years ago; that is, as far as we go back in Natural Hiftory. Now, for this important end, the Doctor has fuggefted, to the Divine as well as to the Philofopher, two grand refources of Nature: the vegetable creation again is one, and the fea, and other great bodies of water, are the other.

As to the former, having found that plants wonderfully thrive in putrid air, he began to attempt, by means of growing vegetables, to purify air that had been injured by animal refpiration and putrefaction; nor was he lefs fuccefsful than before. Thefe plants were fure to recover the air to a degree of fitnefs for breathing in it, and that in proportion to their vigour, and the care he took to remove the rotten leaves

D   and

and branches; which, remaining, would have marred the operation.

WITH regard to the fecond refource of Nature, namely the ocean and other wa‑ ters, Dr. PRIESTLEY having obferved, that both the air corrupted by the breath of animals, and that vitiated by other putrid matter, was in a good meafure fweetened by the feptic part infufing itfelf into water, he concluded, that the fea, the great lakes and rivers, which cover fo large a propor‑ tion of the globe, muft be highly ufeful, by abforbing what is putrid, for the farther purification of the atmofphere: thus be‑ ftowing what would be noxious to man and other animals, upon the formation of marine and other aquatic plants, or upon other purpofes yet unknown.

FROM thefe difcoveries we are affured, that no vegetable grows in vain, but that

from

from the oak of the foreft to the grafs of the field, every individual plant is ferviceable to mankind; if not always diftinguifhed by fome private virtue, yet making a part of the whole which cleanfes and purifies our atmofphere. In this the fragrant rofe and deadly nightfhade co-operate: nor is the herbage, nor the woods that flourifh in the moft remote and unpeopled regions, unprofitable to us, nor we to them; confidering how conftantly the winds convey to them our vitiated air, for our relief, and for their nourifhment. And if ever thefe falutary gales rife to ftorms and hurricanes, let us ftill trace and revere the ways of a beneficent Being; who not fortuitoufly but with defign, not in wrath but in mercy, thus fhakes the waters and the air together, to bury in the deep thofe putrid and peftilential *effluvia*, which the vegetables upon the face of the earth had been infufficient to confume.

THIS,

THIS, GENTLEMEN, is what I had to fay upon the occafion : perhaps too much; but the fruitfulnefs of the fubjeƈt, with my earneſt defire of commemorating fome of the more important experiments and con-clufions of Dr. PRIESTLEY, and of thofe who preceded him in thefe enquiries, will, I hope, plead my excufe. Nor can I con-clude without congratulating this illuſtrious Body, on the poffeffion of fo many mem-bers and friends, fo capable to promote the great ends of this inſtitution ; and who have within thefe few years fo eminently diſtinguiſhed themfelves, by the lights they have thrown, not only upon this, but upon other of the more fubtile fluids of Nature. You will underſtand, that to thefe difco-veries upon faƈtitious air, I join thofe amazing ones upon magnetifm and eleƈtri-city, with all the ufes refulting from them. Here you will recolleƈt the prediƈtion of him, who beſt taught the method of invef-

tigating

tigating philofophical truth, the incompa-
rable Lord BACON, who, with that fpirit
of divination peculiar to exalted genius, affured his difciples, that when men fhould
ceafe to trifle in framing *hypothefes*, and
building hafty fyftems ; and fhould, by a
proper induction from fober and fevere experiments, attain to the knowledge of the
forms of things [their more intimate qualities and laws] ; they fhould in the end command Nature, and perform works as much
greater than were fuppofed practicable by
the powers of natural magic, as the real
actions of a *Cæfar* furpaffed the fictitious
ones of the hero of a romance *. Some
earneft, nor that inconfiderable, of this
magnificent promife this Society has already
obtained. Let thofe who doubt, view that
Needle, which, untouched by any load-
ftone, directs the courfe of the Britifh ma-

* Compare Bac. De Dignit. et Augment. Scient.
lib. iii. cap, 5.

riner

riner round the world ; or that apparatus,
fo perfectly imitating the long fuppofed inimitable lightning; or that other, which
difarms the clouds of that tremendous meteor : or (not to depart from my fubject)
let them fee how Art can, from chalk only,
the leaft promifing fubftance, generate, or
call it unfetter, a copious elaftic fluid im-
prifoned in it, the poifon of man, or his
medicine, according to the mode of application ; which, though invifible, yet dif-
folves earth and metals, and imparts the
fpirit and virtue to the moft prized of mineral waters. Yet thefe are but inventions
of yefterday : I would ftrictly fay, inventions within the memory of my youngeft
hearer. If to thefe late acquifitions, fo
honourable to this Society, I add thofe in
Natural Hiftory, by the zeal and unwearied
attention of fome worthy members, who
have extended your correfpondence, and
adorned your Mufeum ; and by thofe other

gentlemen, who, animated with a noble
fpirit, have, to their lafting honour, under-
taken the moft dangerous and moft diftant
voyages in purfuit of Natural Knowledge :
I fay, when to the progrefs you are
making in Experimental Philofophy, I
add that in the Hiftory of Nature, every
true lover of fcience will rejoice to think,
that your affairs have not, perhaps, at
any period, been in a more flourifhing
condition.

Dr. PRIESTLEY,

IT is now time that, in the name and
by the authority of the Royal Society of
London, inftituted for the improvement of
Natural Knowledge, I prefent you with
this Medal, the palm and laurel of this
Community ; as a faithful and unfading

teftimonial

teftimonial of their regard, and of the juft
fenfe they have of your merit, and of the
perfevering induftry with which you have
promoted the views, and thereby the honour, of this Society. And, in their be-
half, I muft earneftly requeft you, to continue your liberal and valuable inquiries,
whether by farther profecuting this fubject,
probably not yet exhaufted, or by inveftigating the nature of fome other of the
fubtile fluids of the univerfe. You will
remember, that *Fire*, the great inftrument
of the chemifts, is but little known, even
to themfelves; and that it remains a *Query*,
what was by the moft celebrated of philofophers propofed as fuch, whether there be
not a certain fluid (he calls it *Æther*), the
caufe of gravity, the caufe of the various
attractions, and of the animal and vital
motions *. Thefe, Sir, are indeed large
demands: but the Royal Society have

* Newton's Optics, Quer. 18—24.

hitherto

hitherto been fortunate in their pneumatic refearches. And, were it otherwife, they have much to hope from men of your talents and application, and whofe paft labours have been crowned with fo much fuccefs.

A

DISCOURSE

ON THE

TORPEDO;

DELIVERED AT THE

Anniverfary Meeting of the ROYAL SOCIETY,

November 30, 1774.

By Sir JOHN PRINGLE, Bart. PRESIDENT.

PUBLISHED BY THEIR ORDER.

A

DISCOURSE

ON THE

TORPEDO.

GENTLEMEN,

THE difpofal of the annual Prize-medal, founded on the benefaction
of Sir GODFREY COPLEY, Baronet, hav-
ing for fome years paft devolved upon your
Prefident and Council, they have hitherto
been fortunate in executing their truft in
fuch a manner as to receive your approbation.

bation. Indeed, the ſtrict regard for the honour of the Society, and the deference due to the opinions of the other learned Members, have been ſo much the objects of their attention, that they could not well fail to be directed by them to ſuch of your publications, as were moſt deſerving of your favourable notice; and they flatter themſelves, that they ſhall not now be leſs ſucceſsful than on former occaſions. For, if you call to mind the various Papers of Experiments in the laſt volume of your Tranſactions, you may remember, that though you warmly acknowledged the merit of many of them, yet it was with peculiar pleaſure you liſtened to that from Mr. WALSH, upon the Torpedo, on account of the new and very ſtriking circumſtances contained in that communication, and of the pains and time beſtowed by that gentleman on this inquiry.

BUT,

BUT, in order to your more freely feal-
ing the choice of your Council with your
fuffrages, permit me, GENTLEMEN, firft
to lay before you a fhort abftract of what
had been done in this branch of Natural
Hiftory, antecedently to Mr. WALSH's experiments; and then to remind you of a
few of his principal ones, that while we do
juftice to our worthy brother, none may
be defrauded of the praife due to their
labour.

T H E Torpedo, or cramp-fifh, a fpecies
of the ray, being a common inhabitant of
the Mediterranean, was early known to the
Greeks. We find it firft mentioned in a
book anciently afcribed to HIPPOCRATES,
though only as an efculent fifh; but the
name alone (νάρκη) is fufficient to afcertain
the knowledge the ancients then had of its

torporific

torporific qualities. And PLATO, nearly
contemporary with HIPPOCRATES, certainly knew of them, as appears by the
humorous comparifon he makes of SOCRA-
TES to that animal, which he puts into the
mouth of MENON, in his dialogue of that
name. And his celebrated difciple in phyfics, ARISTOTLE, particularly treats of it
in his Hiftory of Animals. The Torpedo
(fays he) hides itfelf in the fand or ooze,
and, whilft the other fifhes fwim over it,
and touch it, he benumbs them, fo as to
catch them and feed upon them : as a
proof, the mullet, the fwifteft of the watery
race, is found in his ftomach.

BUT though ARISTOTLE knew that the
touch of the torpedo ftupified other fifhes,
he feems not to have known that this
extraordinary effect could be tranfmitted
to other animals not in immediate contact
with it, but by the interpofition of a ftick,

a rope,

a rope, or water; facts too curious to have been omitted, had he ever heard of them. Possibly he might have been informed, but rejected the accounts as fabulous (for of all the ancients none appear to have been so much on their guard against impofition); or he might have thrown them into some part, that has been fince loft, of his book called Θαυμάσια 'Ακαςικὰ, *Wonderful Relations.* Yet ARISTOTLE had only the teftimony of fifhermen for what he reports of the torpedo: indeed he exprefsly fays fo. In thofe days, and for many ages after, the pride of Man fet him above experiments; and above the fufpicion, that, by fuch low and mechanical operations, he was to difcover caufes, and learn to reafon. ARISTOTLE himfelf, that admirable genius, knew not this. Had the great Stagyrite heard, that, to underftand by what principles the torpedo acted, a Naturalift from Britain had travelled through Gaul to the Atlantic

E   Ocean,

Ocean, and on that coaſt had made a hun-dred experiments upon that fiſh, and with ſuccefs; there is no doubt but he would have placed that account among the chief of his *Wonderful Relations.* Lord BACON was the firſt who detected and combated this pre-ſumptuous error, and who, by humbling the vanity of man, exalted his power over the works of Nature. He was the firſt who taught, that as *our bread,* ſo our ſcience was to be earned *by the ſweat of our brow;* and the works of this Society will, I truſt, be an everlaſting teſtimony of the truth of his doctrine.

THEOPHRASTUS, the learned ſcholar and ſucceſſor of ARISTOTLE, appears to have been better informed concerning the torpedo than his Maſter. ATHENÆUS relates, that this philoſopher, in his book on venomous animals, obſerved that the torpedo conveyed this benumbing ſenſation

through

through ſticks and ſpears into the hands of the fiſhermen that held them. And ſince I have quoted ATHENÆUS, though not in a chronological order, I ſhall add, that he mentions DIPHILUS of Laodicea, for taking notice, in his commentary upon the *Theriaca* of NICANDER, that it was not the whole, but certain parts of the body of the torpedo, that occaſioned the torpor. HERO of Alexandria, in his Pneumatics, mentions this fiſh as emitting effluvia through braſs and iron, and other ſolid bodies.

PLINY, the laborious and uſeful compiler of ancient natural ſcience, too little a philoſopher himſelf, and too great a lover of the marvellous, has treated this ſubject accordingly. Thus, he ſays, the power of the torpedo may be felt through the length of a rod. or a ſpear, which is a fact; but that this fiſh binds the legs of the nimbleſt perſon that treads upon it, is an exaggera-

tion;

tion ; and that this animal is able to bind the arms of the ſtrongeſt, at a diſtance, is falſe.

Plutarch, though no profeſſed naturaliſt, yet furniſhes us with a fuller and juſter account of the torpedo. According to him, this creature not only benumbs all thoſe that touch it, but alſo ſtrikes a numbneſs through the net into the hands of the liſhermen : nay, as ſome report, if it happen to be laid on the ground, alive, thoſe that pour water upon it ſhall be ſenſible of ſome diminution of their feeling. Now whether this laſt fact has been confirmed by later experiments, I have not learnt; but I am inclined to believe it, as not inconſiſtent with Mr. Walsh's principles. Plutarch adds, that whilſt the torpedo ſwims around his prey, he emits certain effluvia, like darts *, that firſt affect the

* Gr. ὥσπερ βέλη διασπείςει ἀποῤῥοάς.

water,

water, and then the fifhes in it; which, being thus difabled from defending themfelves, or efcaping, are held, as it were, in bonds, or frozen up.

FROM ÆLIAN, who writes a Hiftory of Animals, we might expect more information, on this fubject, than from any other author; but we are much difappointed. He has been fatisfied with reciting a few of the common reports, and adding others, too abfurd to deferve repetition. It is remarkable, that thefe two profeffed writers of Natural Hiftory, PLINY and ÆLIAN, fhould of all the ancients give us the lameft and moft fabulous accounts of this fubject of our inquiry.

PASSING from the philofophers to the phyficians, we fhall receive little more fatisfaction. Before the days of GALEN, the torpedo was applied alive to parts affected,

fected,

fected, and particularly for the cure of an obftinate head-ach, as appears from Scri-bonius Largus, who lived under Clau-dius, and from Dioscorides, who flou-rifhed foon after. But Galen, always reafoning, and oppofing empirical practice, affigns a caufe for that falutary effect. His phyfiological fyftem was in a great meafure founded on the four *primary qualities*, *cold*, *hot*, *wet*, and *dry*. He conceived, there-fore, that the torpedo acted by a frigorific principle; for as cold occafions a numbnefs in an animated body, fo does the fhock given by that fifh. Such were the theory and reafoning of that age ; yet, bad as they were, they prevailed in the fchools of me-dicine upwards of a thoufand years. Ga-len was confirmed in his opinion, by fee-ing, as he himfelf teftifies, that diforder removed by the touch of a living torpedo ; which, being of a cold nature, ftupified or blunted the acute fenfe of pain. The fol-

lowers

lowers of this medical chief improved upon
their leader. A living torpedo not being
always at hand, when a refrigerating medicine was indicated, the deficiency was
fupplied by preparing an oil from the dead
animal, which they were affured muft poffefs all the virtues of the living one. Upon
this conceit, we find PAULUS of Ægina,
one of the ancients of the Galenic fchool,
recommending this oil for tempering the
hot humour of the gout, and for other
ailments that required cooling applications.

Now, confidering what little information we have received from the philofophers and phyficians among the ancients,
it will fcarcely be expected, that we fhould
find more among their poets. Poetry, the
creature of the imagination, can feldom
avail itfelf of ftrict hiftory for a fubject,
whether in the natural or political world.
The hiftorians of either can yet fee but

parts

parts of a great fyftem, and thefe, in appearance, often crooked and deformed,
from not knowing how they are to tally
and to be put together, to compofe the fabric of the univerfc and the hiftory of man.
Such disjointed materials make therefore
but indifferent themes for a bard, whofe
aim is to captivate the fancy with fomething beautiful and finifhcd. In effect,
OPPIAN has made no improvement in the
hiftory of the torpedo, though he contrived
in his *Halieutica* to write an elegant de-
fcription of it, without departing much
from truth. He not only commemorates
the more than poetical powers with which
Nature has endowed this fifh ; but diftin-
guifhcs, like DIPHILUS, the parts where
they peculiarly refide. Thefe parts he calls
λαγόνες (the flanks), from which, as Op-
PIAN imagined, the animal had a faculty
of darting upon other fifhes certain fubftances, he terms κερκίδες, but whereof the
meaning

meaning is obſcure. To the former of theſe expreſſions CLAUDIAN undoubtedly alludes, in a line of thoſe verſes which he copies from OPPIAN, in celebrating the properties of the torpedo :

Sed latus armavit gelido Natura veneno.

BUT, as the Roman Poet has nothing new of his own, I ſhall with him cloſe the relations I have been able to find of this curious fiſh in the monuments of antiquity. We muſt confeſs them to be all unſatisfactory; and the more, as it does not appear that there has been one, GALEN excepted, of all the above-mentioned ancient ſages, who had ever ſeen a living torpedo, much leſs who had made experiments on it ; and, leaſt of all, who had diſſected it. The reſult of their inquiries ſerved for little more than a winter's tale. Such are the accounts that I have been able to collect from the an-cients, concerning this *wonder of the deep* ;

6   omitting

omitting only fuch reports as feemed to be either fuperftitious or fabulous. But of both forts, you may be affured, that, in thofe days of credulity, fo many were impofed on the world, that we are not to wonder, if there have been men of genius and learning, who, not taking the pains to make experiments themfelves, or ftrictly to enquire into thofe made by others, have prefumptuoufly treated the whole affair as a vulgar error.

WITH the fall of the Roman Empire, the hiftory of animals, imperfect as it was, with all other found learning, funk into the darknefs of the times; nor did it emerge before the fixteenth century, an æra ever memorable for the revival of fcience. Then lived and flourifhed BELON, RONDELET, SALVIANI, GESNER, and others, who not only reftored what was anciently known in Natural Hiftory, but greatly improved the fubject,

fubject. Yet experiments were ftill rare and feeble, till, in the next century, HAR-VEY appeared, and began to make them on birds and quadrupeds. Nor did that famous interpreter of Nature finifh his careér, and clofe his eyes in death, before they beheld the rifing ftate of this Society, and the *Academia del Cimento*, our elder but fhort-lived fifter, already formed. Some of the moft eminent of that academy, judging an enquiry into the truth of what had been recorded concerning the torpedo to be an object worthy their attention, availed themfelves of their vicinity to a fea, ftored with that fort of fifh, to make the trials. REDI, one of the moft liberal and enlightened geniufes of that age, began, and was afterwards affifted by BORELLI, and STENO the Dane, his colleagues. Laftly LORENZINI, his fcholar, engaged in the fame purfuit, and publifhed a curious treatife upon the fubject.

REDI's

REDI's firſt ſtep was, by experiments, to diſtinguiſh between the real properties of the torpedo, and ſuch as had erroneouſly been aſcribed to it, by the learned, as well as by the vulgar of former times. To this reſearch he added the anatomy of the ani- mal ; ſo that REDI was alſo the firſt, who with any accuracy deſcribed thoſe crooked ſubſtances, lying on each ſide of the ſpine, near the head, which he conſidered as muſcles (from thence named *muſculi fal- cati)*, that projected certain effluvia, occa- ſioning the ſenſation of numbneſs, more or leſs, as the animal was excited to put theſe organs into action. This hypotheſis, of the tranſmiſſion of effluvia, was immediate- ly embraced by LORENZINI, and after- wards by CLAUDE PERRAULT. But the former, not underſtanding how effluvia could paſs from the body of one animal into that of another, without immediate contact, contradicted, we may ſay, the

evidence

evidence of his fenfes, by denying the fenfation he muft have had upon touching the
torpedo with a ftick, a fpear, or the like
inftrument; unlefs we fhould fuppofe that
thofe fubjects, on which he made his trials,
were too weak for exerting the full energy
of their fpecies.

FROM the like caufes alfo erred the excellent BORELLI. But his theory not admitting the emiffion of benumbing particles, affecting the hand, either in immediate contact with the fifh, or touching it
with a ftick, or the like, he referred the
fenfation to a certain brifk undulation of
the parts touched, which the animal could
excite at will. This action he compared
to that of a ftretched cord, put into quick
vibrations.

INTO a fimilar deception, in the next
generation, fell that ornament of his coun-

try

try and of his age, the excellent M. DE
REAUMUR, upon refuming this fubject.
For, in the year 1714, being on the coaft
of Poitou, he took that opportunity of
making fome new experiments upon the
torpedo, which, with the refult, he communicated to the Royal Academy of Sciences at Paris. His brethren of that illuftrious fociety adopted his hypothefis, as
did indeed the Ingenious over all Europe ;
and fo natural did it appear to them, that
every one wondered it had not been fallen
upon before. What then was this new
fyftem ? In effect, one not very different
from that of BORELLI; for, inftead of the
undefined vibrating parts of the latter,
M. DE REAUMUR fubftituted mufcles (the
mufculi falcati of REDI and LORENZINI),
which, by the vivacity of their action, impreffed on the hand, that touched thefe
parts, a fenfation of numbnefs, owing to
the ftoppage of the progreffion of the

nervous fluid, or a repulfion of the fame.
But, to obviate what might be objected,
the celebrated inveftigator was bound to
deny that this impreffion of numbnefs
could be communicated through water, a
net, or any other foft and yielding fubftance; nay, through a ftick, except a very
fhort one. In fact, M. DE REAUMUR did
deny fuch tranfmiffions; and yet it is certain, that the fhocks from the torpedo are
not lefs conducted through fuch *media*,
than thofe from a charged electrical phial.
Shall we then accufe of want of candour
thofe celebrated authors, BORELLI, LO-
RENZINI, and M. DE REAUMUR? By no
means: but let us lament the weaknefs of
the human intellect, which, prepoffeffed
by fyftem, will often not perceive fuch objects as would ftrike the fenfes of any other
perfon, nay moft certainly their own, in a
more unprejudiced ftate of mind! And let
us regret that other infirmity, fo incident

to

to the beft underftanding, the too great forwardnefs to account for every appearance in Nature, from fuch principles as are known, without confidering how many yet remain to be difcovered! There was a time, and that within the memory of many of my hearers, when thunder and lightning were thought fufficiently accounted for, from fulphureous and nitrous vapours mixing with the air. At prefent, we doubt of the exiftence of fuch vapours in the atmofphere, and are otherwife fure, that the electrical fluid only is concerned in the formation of that meteor. Now it feems this very fluid is the efficient caufe of the amazing qualities of the torpedo. Nothing could be more unexpected, yet perhaps nothing more true.

THE difcovery of the Leyden Phial opened a wide and rich field for the advancement of philofophy; and to the honour

nour of this Society it will ever be re-
membered, how much they have availed
themfelves of that fortunate accident, for
interpreting fome of the more intricate
phænomena of Nature. A few years after
that memorable event, the celebrated profeffor ALLAMAND, Fellow of this Society,
hearing of a fifh, in the Dutch fettlement
of Surinam, refembling a congre-eel, but
with properties fimilar to thofe of the torpedo, engaged his friend M. 's GRAVE-
SANDE, governor of Effequebo, to make
the enquiry. That gentleman readily complied; and, in the year 1754, wrote M.
ALLAMAND a letter on the fubject, which
was foon after publifhed in the fecond volume of the Tranfactions of the Society at
Haerlem. M. 's GRAVESANDE fays, that
the experiment was made on a fpecies of
eel, the Dutch call *fidder-vis (tremble-fifh)*,
and that it produced the fame effects with
electricity, with which he had been well

F   acquainted,

acquainted, by having, with his learned corre-
fpondent, made many experiments with the
electrical phial; nay, that the fhocks from the
fifh were much more violent, if it happened
to be ftrong and lively of its kind ; for then
it would infallibly throw the perfon who
touched it to the ground. But M. 's
GRAVESANDE adds, that fuch exertions,
in this animal, were accompanied with no
fparks of fire, as in an electrical machine.
Thus far I have abridged M. 's GRAVE-
SANDE's Letter. M. ALLAMAND fubjoins,
that he was fatisfied that this eel muft be a
fpecies of the gymnotus of ARTEDI ; and
all our fubfequent accounts have confirmed
his opinion.

IN the fecond part of the fixth volume
of the fame valuable Work, we find, of the
fame animal, a more ample relation extracted from fome Letters of M. VANDER
LOTT, dated from Rio Effequebo, 1761.

This

This gentleman makes two fpecies, the black and the reddifh, though he acknow-ledges, that, excepting the difference of colour and degree of ftrength, they are not materially different. In moft of the expe-riments with thefe animals, M. VANDER LOTT remarked a wonderful fimilitude between them and an electrical apparatus: nay, he obferved, that the fhock could be given to the finger of a perfon, held at fome diftance from the bubble of air, form-ed by this eel, when it rifes to the furface of the water in order to breathe; and he concluded, that at fuch times the electrical matter was difcharged from its lungs. He mentions another characterizing circum-ftance; which is, that though metals, in general, were conductors to its electrical fluid, yet fome were found to be fenfibly better than others for that purpofe.

ABOUT the fame time that M. 's GRAVE-SANDE made his difcovery in America,

M. ADAN-

M. ADANSON, an eminent French naturalift, met with the fame, or a fimilar fifh,
in the river of Senegal in Africa. He takes
notice, that this animal had little relation
to any of the known inhabitants of the
water; that its body was round, and without fcales, like an eel, but much thicker in
proportion to its length; that it was well
known to the natives, and that the French
called it *trembleur*, from the effects it produced; not fo much a numbnefs, like that
arifing from the torpedo, as a very painful
trembling in the limbs of thofe who touched it. He adds, that this effect did not
fenfibly differ from the fhock given by the
Leyden Phial, which he had felt; and that
it was communicated, in the fame manner,
by fimple contact, or by the interpofition
of a ftick, or an iron rod (five or fix
feet long), fo as to force the perfon to
drop whichever of them he had in his
hand.

M. FERMIN,

M. FERMIN, in his Natural Hiftory of
Surinam, publifhed at Amfterdam in 1765,
obferves of a fifh, which the Dutch there
call *Beef-aal (tremble-eel)*, that one cannot
touch it with the hands, or even with a
ftick, without feeling a horrible numbnefs
in the arms, up to the fhoulders. And he
farther relates, that, making fourteen perfons join each other by the hands, whilft
he grafped the hand of the laft with one of
his, and with the other touched the eel
with a ftick, the whole number felt fo violent a fhock, that he could not prevail on
them to repeat the experiment. This fifh,
I believe, we may with probability fay,
was the fame fpecies of gymnotus defcribed
by M. 's GRAVESANDE and M. VANDER
LOTT, though the Author does not compare its operations to thofe of the electrical
phial.

THE earlieft account, for a diftinct one, that I have met with of this kind of eel, in that quarter of the world, is by M. RICHER, the aftronomer, recorded by M. DU HA- MEL, in his Hiftory of the Royal Acade- my of Sciences, for the year 1677. In the ifland of Cayenne, where M. RICHER had made his obfervations, there is a fifh, fays M. DU HAMEL, not unlike a congre- eel, which, touched with the finger, or even with the end of a ftick, affects the arm with a numbnefs, nay the head with a giddinefs, and the eyes with a dimnefs of fight, which M. RICHER had himfelf felt upon making the experiment.

IF any farther evidence were wanting, to afcertain the electrical nature of this eel, in thofe parts, I would recommend the perufal of the Effay on the Natural Hiftory of Guiana, by Dr. BANCROFT, Member

of

of this Society, where the reader will find feveral curious experiments made on this animal by that gentleman. But, as the book is in every body's hands, I fhall only take notice, that the Author confirms M. VANDER LOTT's account, of a fhock from this animal being communicated through a confiderable fpace of air ; a circumftance to which we have nothing fimilar in the tor-pedo, though it be a common effect in an electrical difcharge.

I SHALL not, therefore, GENTLEMEN, take up more of your time, with offering you farther accounts of thefe curious ani-mals, given us by travellers ; and the lefs, as I have met with no original ones, ex-cepting the above, but what, from either too much brevity, or manifeft figns of in-accuracy, have left much doubt to what *genera* of fifhes thofe electrical ones were to be referred. I fhould only except that eel,

F 4   which

which M. DE LA CONDAMINE defcribes
in his voyage down the River of Amazons,
that was moft probably the true electrical
gymnotus (fo commonly found in the rivers of the adjacent country of Guiana),
about which we have been juft difcourfing.
Not fo that fifh which Mr. MOORE found
in an African lake near the Gambia ; nor
that other, which Mr. ATKINS faw in the
river Sierra-leon, likewife, in Africa. And
it is pretty evident that the electrical fifh,
mentioned and delineated, but fcarcely defcribed, by NIEUHOF, as taken in fome of the
lakes of India, and called by the Dutch *meer-
aal (lake-cel)*, is no fpecies of the gymnotus,
at leaft if juftly drawn ; fince we find there
a long fin on the back of that creature, and
none on its belly. No more fhould that
fifh, provided with torporific powers, which
PISO found in Brazil, have any other relation to the gymnotus, fince the Author
compares it in figure to a fole : nor that
other,

other, of the fame country, poffeffed of fimilar qualities, which Piso calls *Piraqué*
(Margraf, *Puraqué*), if it at all refem-
bled the figures given of it by thefe travellers and natural hiftorians. I would pafs
the fame judgment upon the Indian *congrus*
monftrofus of Bontius. And I fhould
hefitate about that eel, the fubject of a
Paper communicated to this Society in the
year 1680, by Dr. Gale, from the author
Mr. Bateman, who had been twenty
years a planter in Surinam. All that I
would with any degree of certainty conclude, is, that, among fifhes, the electrical
properties are not confined to that fpecies
of ray called the torpedo, nor to that fpecies of gymnotus called the *gymnotus electri-*
cus; but that Nature has endowed with the
fame powers feveral other inhabitants of
the waters, though hitherto imperfectly
known.

Now,

Now, in juſtice to thoſe authors who
have firſt mentioned the electric gymnotus,
and eſpecially to thoſe who have originally
ſurmiſed a ſimilitude between the properties of the torpedo and thoſe of that electrical eel, and between the properties of both
and thoſe of the Leyden Phial, I have
thought proper to commemorate their
names on this occaſion ; though, after all,
I have reaſon to believe that our worthy
Brother has taken the hint of making his
experiments from none of them, but ſolely
from what he had read concerning the torpedo in writers, who thought of nothing
leſs than referring ſuch powers in animals
to an electrical origin ; nay, who lived,
many of them, long before the laws of
electricity were known. Nor had the ſur-
prizingly benumbing effects of the electric
gymnotus ever been ſo narrowly obſerved,
much leſs confronted with an electrical apparatus, as that we could with any preciſion

fion fay, how far Nature had carried the analogy between the two.

To Mr. WALSH, therefore, we owe not only the firft, but a numerous fet of the beft chofen experiments on the torpedo, for afcertaining its electrical nature, together with fome correct and elegant drawings of the entire animal, and of fome of its principal organs that appeared upon diffection. For this latter part of the difquifition, the Society, as well as Mr. WALSH, is much beholden to another Member, Mr. JOHN HUNTER, who thereby has fupplied us with an ufeful addition to the anatomical examination of the animal by REDI, STENO, and LORENZINI. And I may moreover acquaint you, that, though Mr. WALSH has laid before us an account of his principal experiments, his occupations have not yet permitted him to enumerate every curious particular that occurred to

him

him in the courfe of his refearch ; as I can teftify, from having been favoured with the perufal of the journal he had kept of all his tranfactions.

THE very firft experiment of Mr. WALSH difcovered the electrical quality of that fluid in the torpedo (which had fo long diftinguifhed this fifh), by his conveying it through the fame conductors with electricity, fuch as metals, water, and animal fluids ; and by intercepting it by the fame non-conductors, namely, glafs and fealing-wax. Nor in this circumftance only did the fimilitude between the electric and torpedinous fluids appear : one of the moft brilliant of Mr. WALSH's difcoveries was, that this animal not only could accumulate in one part a large quantity of electric matter, but was furnifhed with a certain organization difpofed in the manner of the Leyden Phial. Thus, while one furface of

the

the electric part (fuppofe on the back) was charged with this matter, or, as it is called, was in a pofitive ftate, the other furface (that on the belly) was deprived of it, or was in a negative ftate ; fo that the equilibrium could be reftored, by making a communication between the two furfaces, by water, the fluids of the human body, or metals. A man, preffing upon one of thefe furfaces with one hand, could, with the other, by the mediation of his own fluids, make a circuit for the conveyance, and at the fame inftant receive a fhock ; viz. the fame fenfation that is impreffed by the electric matter in paffing through our arms and body, from the infide of a charged Leyden Phial to its outward coating. We need but attend to the following experiment, which Mr. WALSH made at Rochelle, in prefence of the Academy there, to fee how admirable this circuit is, and how fimilar to a common electrical one. A

living

living torpedo was laid on a table, upon a
wet napkin; round another table ftood five
perfons infulated; and two brafs wires,
each thirteen feet long, were fufpended
from the cieling by filken ftrings. One of
the wires refted by one end on the wet
napkin; the other end was immerfed in a
bafon full of water, placed on a fecond
table, on which ftood four other bafons,
likewife full of water. The firft perfon
put a finger of one hand into the water in
which the wire was immerfed, and a finger
of the other hand into the fecond, and fo
on fucceffively till all the five perfons communicated with one another by the water
in the bafons. In the laft bafon one end of
the fecond wire was dipped, and with the
other end Mr. WALSH touched the back of
the torpedo, when the five perfons felt a
fhock, differing in nothing from that of the
Leyden experiment, except in being weak-
er. Mr. WALSH, who was not in the
circle

circle of conduction, felt nothing. This was feveral times fuccefsfully repeated, even with eight perfons; and the experiment being related by M. DE SEIGNETTE, mayor of the city, and one of the fecretaries of the Academy of Sciences of Rochelle, and publifhed by him in the French Gazette, the account becomes the more authenticated. For though we place full confidence in the candour and veracity of our worthy Brother, yet, in the eyes of the Public, the evidence muft be ftrengthened by the teftimony of thofe, who, but for the fake of truth and fcience, were no wife interefted in the matter. We are therefore the more obliged to Mr. WALSH, for having made thefe experiments *not in a corner*, but I may fay, before the world; and in that very country which gave birth to the celebrated M. DE REAUMUR, whofe reputation as a philofopher could not but fuffer fome diminution, in proportion to

5   the

the credit gained at this time by the fortunate ftranger. And indeed the whole behaviour of the learned academicians, firft
at Rochelle, and afterwards at Paris (when
the experiments became known there) was
fuch to their gueft, as fhewed them to be
on this, as on other occafions, the true
lovers of fcience, emulous, not envious, of
the reputation of their neighbours.

BUT though no farther evidence be
wanting to authenticate the experiments of
Mr. WALSH, yet, for the confirmation of
the conclufions he draws from them, it is
with pleafure that I can join the teftimony
of our learned and candid Brother, Dr.
INGENHOUSZ, phyfician to their Imperial
Majefties at Vienna, who, being in Italy
when he received a general account of Mr.
WALSH's fuccefs, at my requeft repaired
to Leghorn, to make fome experiments
himfelf upon the torpedo. How far they

agreed

agreed with, and corroborated thofe of Mr. WALSH, I need not mention, as you have fo lately heard the Doctor's Letter to me on that fubject.

NOR fhall I return to enter into any far-ther detail of Mr. WALSH's experiments, confidering what encroachment I have already made on your time, and how fenfible you muft be, that thofe which I have already reminded you of, have merited the honours you are now conferring upon him. I fhall only obferve, that our ingenious Brother having traced the fimilitude between the operations of the torpedo and thofe of an electrical apparatus, he found it fo ftrong, as to perfuade him that it was the identical fluid that actuated both the animal and the machine. Yet he remarks, that, though the charged phial occafions attraction and repulfion in fuch light bodies as the pith-balls, placed near it, and its

G   difcharge

difcharge is obtained through a fpace of air, and accompanied with light and found; nothing of this occurs with refpeƈt to the torpedo. But to thefe objeƈtions againft a perfeƈt agreement between the eleƈtrical and torpedinous fluids, Mr. WALSH an-fwers, that, upon charging a number of large jars with a fmall quantity of eleƈtric matter, and then difcharging them, that matter will yield the appearances of the torpedo only. It will not now pafs the hundredth part of that inch of air, which in its colleƈted ftate it would run through with eafe; the fpark and fnap and the at-traƈtion and repulfion of the balls will alfo be wanting; nor will a point, brought however near, if not juft in contaƈt, be able to draw off the charge; and yet this diffufed eleƈtric matter, to effeƈt its equili-brium, will inftantaneoufly pafs through a confiderable circuit of different conduƈtors properly conneƈted, and give a fenfible

4   fhock

fhock to fuch perfons as compofe the circle.
But where is that large furface of diffufed
electricity to be found in the torpedo? Mr.
WALSH replies, that from a minute divi-
fion of parts a large furface will arife; and
that even our naked eye will tell us, that
thofe fingular tubulated organs of the torpedo confift, like our electric batteries, of
many bodies of a prifmatic form, whofe
furfaces, taken together, compofe a confiderable area. To this argument we may
add, that hitherto no difference has been
found, excepting with regard to more and
lefs, between the electric matter which is
drawn from the clouds, and that other
which pervades all terreftrial bodies, and is
collected by every apparatus. If therefore
between lightning itfelf, and the charge of
a Leyden Phial, there is no fpecific difference, nay fcarcely a variety, as far as is
known, why then fhould we unneceffarily
multiply fpecies, and fuppofe the torpedo

provided

provided with one different from that which is every where elſe to be found? But leaving this queſtion to be more thoroughly handled by ſubſequent experiments, let us conclude, that ſuch has been the ſimilitude eſtabliſhed between the electrical fluid of the torpedo, and that of Nature at large, that, in a phyſical ſenſe, they may be conſidered as preciſely the ſame.

Mr. Hunter has well obſerved, and I think he is the firſt who has made the obſervation, that the magnitude and number of the nerves beſtowed on theſe electric organs, in proportion to their ſize, muſt appear as extraordinary as their effects; and that, if we except the important organs of our ſenſes, there is no part even of the moſt perfect animal, which, for its ſize, is more liberally ſupplied with nerves; nor yet do theſe nerves of the electric organs ſeem neceſſary for any ſenſation that can belong to them.

them. And with refpect to action, he obferves, that there is no part of any animal,
however ftrong and conftant its action may
be, which enjoys fo large a proportion of
them. If then it be probable, that thefe
nerves are unneceffary for the purpofe either
of fenfation or action, may we not conclude
that they are fubfervient to the formation,
collection, and management of the electrical fluid, efpecially as it appears, from Mr.
WALSH's experiments, that the will of the
animal commands the electric powers of its
body ?

If thefe reflections be juft, we may with
fome probability foretell, that no difcovery
of confequence will ever be made by future
phyfiologifts, concerning the nature of the
nervous fluid, without acknowledging the
lights they have borrowed from the experiments of Mr. WALSH upon the living torpedo, and the diffection of the dead animal

G 3   by

by Mr. HUNTER. But whether this will
be the individual effect or not, philofophy,
by thefe curious and fuccefsful refearches,
has made a valuable acquifition; fince we
may be affured, that whatever tends to dif-
clofe the *caufæ rerum*, the fecret laws of
Nature, cannot ultimately fail of fubjecting
her, more or lefs, to the ufes of life; and
of manifefting, more and more, the wifdom and power of the Creator in all his
works,

MR. WALSH,

IN confequence of the approbation of
the choice made by the Council, fo un-
feignedly expreffed in the countenance of
every gentleman prefent, it remains that,
in the name and by the authority of the
Royal Society of London, formed for the
improvement

improvement of Natural Knowledge, I deliver into your hand this Medal, the prize
you have fo meritorioufly obtained ; not
doubting, SIR, of your grateful acceptance
of fo honourable and unperifhing a memorial of their efteem, and of the fenfe of
their obligations to a perfon, who, in fo
diftinguifhed a manner, has contributed to
promote the great ends of their inftitution.
And, in the fame refpectable name, let me
add, that they are fo much perfuaded of
your abilities to affift in their grand work,
the *Interpretation of Nature*, that they earneftly call upon you to continue your liberal and fpirited labours. With pleafure
they underftand that you have already
turned your views to the electric gymnotus, that other wonder of the waters, an
animal poffeffed of powers fimilar to thofe
of the torpedo, but of fuperior energy ;
and the Society flatter themfelves, that fo
much light will be gained by that inquiry,

that

that you will be enabled foon to make a
farther difcovery of the myfteries of Nature. Her veil fear not, SIR, to approach *.
Animated with the prefence of this illuftrious and fuccefsful Body, I will venture to
affirm, that Nature has no veil, but what
time and perfevering experiments may remove. In the inftance before us, view the
progrefs of the powers of the mind ; view
the philofophers of the early ages, like the
" children of the world †," amufed and
fatisfied with the ftories of the torpedo ; as
incurious about their authenticity, as about
the caufes of fuch extraordinary effects.
This animal ferved them for an emblem,
or an hieroglyphic, for a figure of fpeech,
or an allufion of pleafantry ; at beft as a
theme for a copy of verfes. But the

* Alluding to that paffage in Mr. WALSH's Paper,
" We here approach to that veil of Nature, which
" Man cannot remove."

† Lord BACON.

World,

World, rifing in years and in wifdom, re-
jects fuch trifles. The Interpreters of Nature, in the adult ftate of Time, make
experiments and inductions, diftruft their
intellects, confide in facts and in their
fenfes : and by thefe arts drawing afide
the veil of Nature, find a mean and gro-
veling animal armed with lightning, that
awful and celeftial fire, revered by the ancients as the peculiar attribute of the father
of their gods.

A

D I S C O U R S E

ON THE

ATTRACTION of MOUNTAINS;

DELIVERED AT THE

Anniverſary Meeting of the ROYAL SOCIETY,
November 30, 1775.

By Sir JOHN PRINGLE, Bart. PRESIDENT.

PUBLISHED BY THEIR ORDER.

A

D I S C O U R S E

ON THE

ATTRACTION OF MOUNTAINS.

GENTLEMEN,

T HE fatisfaction you difcovered when
a propofal was laid before you, *for*
meafuring the attraction of mountains, and
the manner in which you received the account of what had been done to fulfil that
view, were fuch indications of your applaufe, that your Council, ever attentive to
your

your fentiments, have adjudged the Prize-
medal of this year to the Reverend NEVIL
MASKELYNE, his Majefty's Aftronomer at
Greenwich, the author and conductor of
that experiment. The many and valuable
communications of our worthy Brother,
preceding this inquiry, you have never
failed to diftinguifh : but thefe his late
labours, undertaken at your requeft, with
their fuccefsful refult, related in his Paper,
intitled, *Obfervations made on the Mountain
Schehallien for finding its Attraction*, and
inferted in the fecond part of the volume
of your Tranfactions for this year, feemed
to lay the Society under fuch obligations,
as your Council prefumed you could not
otherwife exprefs than by the higheft mark
of your approbation. In confequence of
this reflection, I have, by their authority,
caufed Mr. MASKELYNE's name, with the
date of the prefent year, to be engraven on
the Medal, in order to perpetuate to him
the

the honour you were this day to confer
upon him; if, after allowing me to recal
to your remembrance fome of the more interefting particulars of this difquifition, and
his operations, you fhould not refufe your
fanction to the judgment of your Council.

I shall not confider the fubject of attraction at large, nor touch upon any fpecies of it, excepting what in latter times,
by the effects, has been diftinguifhed by
the name of *gravity* or *gravitation;* a property of bodies, perceptible to the vulgar,
when things fall to the ground, but long
acknowledged by this Society, to be a quality impreffed by the Creator on all matter,
whether of the earth or of the heavens,
whether at reft or in motion: *He commanded, and it was created.*

THE difcovery of this extenfive principle, the phyfics of aftronomy, depended

upon a juft notion of the arrangement and
motions of the fpheres ; for, to underftand
their œconomy, it was neceffary previoufly
to know, which of the ftars were quiefcent,
which moved, and in what manner. Whoever therefore found out the true celeftial
fyftem, might be faid to have paved the
way to the knowledge of that fublime truth,
the law by which the natural world is go-
verned. But who were the inventors here ?
Were they Chaldeans or Ægyptians ? Was
it PYTHAGORAS, or PHILOLAUS, or any
other Greek, either in their own country,
or tranfplanted to the mathematical fchools
of Alexandria ? I fhall not enter upon that
enquiry, as fruitlefs as obfcure. All that is
clear and to our purpofe, is, that fome of
the ancient Greeks conjectured rightly
about the ftability of the Sun, and the circular motion of the earth ; but this was
never a general perfuafion, nor does it feem
to have been mentioned any more after the

7   age

age of PTOLEMY, who in the fecond century did not fo much invent a new fyftem,
as adopt that which now goes under his
name, the prevailing one of his time, and
nearly the fame with that of ARISTOTLE.
This, though erroneous, was not, perhaps,
incapable of improvements from celeftial
obfervations ; but when the philofophy of
the fchools was united with the Ptolemaic
hypothefis, and both were fubjected to ju-
dicial aftrology, then was aftronomy de-
bafed to the level of the pretended learning
of the dark ages that enfued, and increafed
their darknefs.

BUT at the appointed time, when it
pleafed the Supreme Difpenfer of every
good gift to reftore light to a bewildered
world, and more particularly to manifeft
his wifdom in the fimplicity as well as in
the grandeur of his works, he opened the
glorious fcene with the revival of a found

H   aftronomy.

aftronomy. COPERNICUS of Thorn (a Polifh city in the Regal Pruffia), endowed by Nature with excellent talents, improved by a fuperior degree of mathematics, and by travelling, became, early in life, difgufted with the contradictions about the caufe of the celeftial phænomena. He had recourfe, as he himfelf informs us *, to every author upon the fubject, to fee whether any had been more confiftent in explaining the irregular motions of the ftars, than the mathematical fchools; but received no fatisfaction, till firft, from CICERO, he found that NICETAS had maintained the motion of the earth; and next, from PLUTARCH, that others of the ancients had been of the fame opinion. CICERO had faid that ' NICETAS the Syracufan (accord-' ing to THEOPHRASTUS) held that the ' heavens, the fun, the moon, the ftars, in'

---

* Præf. ad Lib. de Revolutionibus Orbium Cœleftium.

' a word,

' a word, all the celeftial bodies, ftood ftill,
' and that, excepting the earth, nothing
' moved in the world; but that, whilft
' the earth with the greateft celerity turned
' round its axis, the fame phænomena
' were produced as if it ftood ftill, and the
' heavens moved. And this fome thought
' was alfo PLATO's notion, but fomewhat
' obfcurely expreffed *.'

PLUTARCH's words were, ' Others fup-
' pofe the earth to be at reft; but PHILO-
' LAUS, the Pythagorean, that it is carried
' in the ecliptic round the fire, like the
' fun and the moon. HERACLIDES of
' Pontus, and ECPHANTUS the Pythago-
' rean, make the earth move like a wheel
' about its centre, from weft to eaft, but
' not to change its place †.

* Cicer. Quæft. Academic.
† Placit. Philof. lib. iii. cap. 3.

[100]

FROM thefe quotations, and what Co-
PERNICUS farther fays *, we find how
little difpofed that great man was to plume
himfelf with the inventions of others: nay,
he was rather anxious not only to do juftice to thofe who had gone before him,
but by their authority to fcreen himfelf
from the cenfure of innovation, abfurdity,
and impiety, that awaited the publication
of his doctrine. After all, the original
genius of COPERNICUS was but little beholden, for the difcovery of thofe fublime
truths, to either NICETAS or PLATO,
fince it appears, from CICERO, that thefe
two believed both the moon and the planets to be motionlefs. Nor could he be
more affifted by PHILOLAUS, who taught
that *the earth turned round* a *fire ;* but this
fire could not be the fun, becaufe that Ancient compares the motion of the earth
about *the fire,* to the revolution of the fun

* Placit. Philof. lib. iii. cap. 3.

and

and moon about the earth. Laſtly, what little light Copernicus could draw from Heraclides and Ecphantus, I ſcarcely need ſay, ſince they, though admitting the diurnal motion of the earth, denied the annual.

But if Copernicus ſought to do juſtice, why did he not rather cite a clear and exprefs paſſage in the Arenarius of Archimedes, for the fixed ſtate of the ſun, and for the motion of the earth in a circle round his body? ' What moſt philoſophers ' call the world,' ſays that famous Ancient, ' is a ſphere, of which the centre is that of ' the earth, and whereof the ſemi-diameter ' is equal to a right line joining the centers ' of the earth and the ſun. But Aris- ' tarchus the Samian, refuting this opi- ' nion, has advanced an hypotheſis, where- ' by the world ſhould be many times ' greater than what is here ſaid; for he

H 3   ' ſuppoſes

' fuppofes that the fixed ftars and the fun
' remain immoveable, and that the earth
' is carried in a circle round the fun, placed
' in the middle of its courfe *.'

THUS far ARCHIMEDES, who feems not
to difapprove the fyftem, but who explains
it no farther, as what he had quoted was
fufficient for his purpcfe. It is probable
that the penetrating genius of ARISTAR-
CHUS had difcovered the true arrangement
of all the celeftial bodies, and thereby totally anticipated COPERNICUS ; but that
circumftance is no where, that I know of,
recorded ; and otherwife, we fhould acquit
our illuftrious Reformer of plagiarifm, with
regard to ARISTARCHUS, fince neither the
Arenarius of ARCHIMEDES, where that
paffage is found, nor indeed any other of
his valuable remains, had feen the light
before the death of COPERNICUS. This

* Archimed. Arenar. ed. Oxon. 1676.

5   extraordinary

extraordinary perfon had, even before the meridian of life, completed his difcoveries, and comprifed them in his book *De Revo-lutionibus Orbium Cælcftium*, his only work; but which he had prudently fuppreffed, till he had maturely confidered his fubject, and had found a neceffary and powerful patron, the pope himfelf, PAUL III., a lover of aftronomy, to protect him. Alluding to the admonition of the Poet, he tells the Pontiff, ' he had fuffered that fruit of ' his labours to ripen, not nine years only, ' but four times nine *.' Confenting at laft to the publication, he committed the care of the impreffion to fome friends in a diftant city, from whom he received the finifhed copy a few hours before he expired †.

FEW compofitions have deftroyed more riveted errors, or eftablifhed more import-

* Præfat. ad Lib. de Revolut.
† Gaffend. in Vita Copernic.

ant

ant truths. Here, inftead of an abfolute
ftate of reft for the earth, its triple motion
is afcertained, the diurnal about its axis,
the annual about the fun, and that other,
known by the term *preceffion of the equi-
noxes*; all which, till then, had been referred to the motion of the heavens. He
likewife demonftrated the double orbit of
the moon; that is, her menftrual motion
about the earth, and her annual about the
fun. Nor did the wife COPERNICUS ftop
here: for, after laying this folid foundation
of the celeftial phyfics, he began the fuperftructure, by furmifing a principle of *attraction* to be inherent in all matter. Thus,
in refuting the peripatetic notion, that bodies fall to the ground, becaufe, by a law
of Nature, every thing heavy tends to the
centre of the univerfe (which they fuppofed
to be in the centre of the earth), he obferved that ' the earth could not be the
' centre of the orbits of feveral of the pla-
' nets,

' nets, becaufe of the apparent irregulari-
' ties of their motions, and therefore could
' not be the centre of the univerfe. Hence,
' according to thefe philofophers, there
' muft be more centres than one; and if
' fo, who could tell the true centre, toward
' which all bodies were to gravitate? As
' for gravity (fays he), I confider it as
' nothing more than a certain natural ap-
' petence *(appetentia)*, that the Creator
' has impreffed upon all the parts of mat-
' ter, in order to their uniting and coa-
' lefcing into a globular form, for their
' better prefervation; and it is credible
' that the fame power is alfo inherent in
' the fun, and moon, and planets, that
' thofe bodies likewife may conftantly re-
' tain that round figure in which we be-
' hold them *.' Farther, COPERNICUS
looked upon the fun as the chief governing
power of the earth and all the other pla-

* De Revolut. Orb. Cœleft. lib. i. cap. 9.

nets;

nets ; for, after placing the great luminary in the centre, he cries out with rapture, ' *Profecto tanquam in folio regali fol refidens* ' *circumagentem gubernat aftrorum fami-* ' *liam* *.' Nor was this *government* under-ftood to be exercifed by any other power than that of *attraction ;* as may be inferred from fome of the laft words of the cele-brated TYCHO BRAHE, who, perceiving the approach of death, called for the fa-mous KEPLER (then a young man, and his affiftant in his obfervatory at Prague), and after charging him with completing and publifhing the aftronomical tables which he was leaving unfinifhed, thus ad-dreffed him : ' My friend, although what ' I afcribe to a voluntary, and, as it were, ' an obfequious motion of the planets ' round the fun, you attribute to an *at-* ' *tractive* energy of that body ; yet I muft ' entreat you, that, in the publication of

---

* De Revolut. Orb. Cæleft. lib. i. cap. 10.

' my

' my obfervations, you would explain all
' the celeftial motions by my hypothefis,
' rather than by that of COPERNICUS,
' which I know you would otherwife in-
' cline to follow *.

FROM this paffage, which I have taken
from the life of TYCHO BRAHE, it would
feem, that though that other excellent
aftronomer was not infenfible of fome in-
fluencing power of the fun over the planets,
he would not however exprefs it by fo
ftrong a term as *attraction*. But in what
manner KEPLER complied with the requeft
of his dying patron, it is not our prefent
purpofe to mention, and therefore we fhall
only obferve, that in his own works he
conftantly maintains the doctrine of attraction, and carries it even farther than ever
COPERNICUS had done. Thus he calls
gravity *a corporeal and mutual affection*

* Gaffend. in Vit. Tych. Brah. cap. 5.

between

*between fimilar bodies, in order to their
union* *. Again he remarks with COPER-
NICUS, againſt the peripatetics, that ' hea-
' vy bodies do not tend to the centre of
' the univerſe, but to the centre of thoſe
' larger round bodies, of which they make
' a part; ſo that, if the earth were not
' ſpherical, things would not fall from all
' points towards its centre. If a ſtone
' were to be placed at a diſtance from ano-
' ther ſtone, in any part of the univerſe,
' without the ſphere of action of a third
' body, like two magnets, they would
' come together in ſome intermediate point,
' each advancing, in ſpace, in the inverſe
' proportion of their quantities of matter.
' Hence, if the moon and the earth were
' not by ſome power kept aſunder in their
' reſpective orbits, they would move to-
' wards one another; the moon making
' fifty-three parts of the way, while the

* Aſtron. Nov. in Introduct.

' earth

' earth made one, fuppofing their denfities
' equal *.'

FROM the fame principle KEPLER accounted for the general motion of the
tides; to wit, by the attraction of the
moon, and exprefsly calls it *virtus tractoria
quæ in luna eft* †. He adds, that if the
earth did not exert an attractive power
over its own waters, they would rife and
rufh to the moon ‡. Farther, we find him
fufpecting certain irregularities in the motion of the moon to be owing to the combined action of the earth and fun upon its
body §. Thefe, and other reflections concerning the univerfality of attraction, he
accompanies with an ingenious anticipation
of a law of Nature, from conjecture only,
but which was afterwards made out by experiments. The fchools had taught, that

---

* Aftron. Nov. in Introduct.   † Ibid.
‡ Ibid.   § Aftron. Nov. cap. xxxvii.

' fome

' fome bodies were by their nature heavy,
' and fo fell to the ground, and that others
' were by their nature light, and therefore
' mounted upwards:' but KEPLER pronounced that ' no bodies whatfoever were
' abfolutely light, but only relatively fo ;
' and, confequently, that all matter was
' fubjected to the law of gravitation *.'

HITHERTO the genius of KEPLER had
been fortunate, in tracing out that great
principle, which hindered the planets from
flying off from the fun : But what kept
them from falling into that mafs of fire,
and what power perpetuated their motion
in their orbits ? Here his fagacity had
failed him, and left his imagination to
furnifh the idea of a fyftem of *vortices* for
DESCARTES.

BUT howfoever incomplete thefe notions
were concerning gravitation, yet, in juftice

* Aftron. Nov. in Introduct.

to their diſtinguiſhed authors, COPERNI-
CUS and KEPLER, I thought proper to
commemorate them on this occaſion, as
none before them had expreſſed themſelves
ſo fully, and with ſo much truth, on that
curious ſubjeἀ : and as none, from their
days to thoſe of Dr. HOOKE, made any
ſuch improvement, as would apologize for
my taking up ſo much more of your time
in recalling their ſentiments to your remembrance, let it ſuffice to mention,
that the firſt who, in this country, embraced that doἀrine, was Dr. GILBERT *,
but who did not properly diſtinguiſh between attraἀion and magnetiſm ; and that
the next was Lord BACON, who, though
not a convert to the *Copernican* ſyſtem, yet
acknowledged an attraἀive power in matter †. In France, we find FERMAT and

* De Magnetc.

† Nov. Organ. lib. ii. aphor. 36. 45. 48. Sylv.
Sylvar. cent. i. exp. 33.

ROBERVAL,

ROBERVAL, mathematicians of great eminence, of the fame opinion *; and in Italy,
BORELLI, after GALILEO †, who was the
firſt in that country who conceived that
idea, but far from that preciſion and exten-
ſion we find it in his contemporaries BA-
CON and KEPLER.

BEFORE we paſs from KEPLER, it will
be proper to obſerve, that this great im-
prover of aſtronomy did not, perhaps, after
all, contribute ſo much to the advancement
of this theory, by thoſe conjectures which
I have related, as by ſome aſtronomical deductions from TYCHO BRAHE's obſervations, ſince known by the name of KEP-
LER's *Laws*. The firſt was, that the planets move not in circular, but in elliptical
orbits, of a ſmall eccentricity, whereof the
centre of the ſun makes one of its *foci*.

* Montucla Hiſt. des Mathem. part iv. liv. viii.
† Syſt. Coſmic.

The

The fecond, that the fame planet defcribes about the fun equal areas in equal times. The third, that in different planets, the fquares of the periodic times are as the cubes of their mean diftances from the fun.

Such were the preparatives to the true philofophy, and indeed excellent materials for the architect then unborn. But till Sir Isaac Newton appeared, notwithftanding the numerous and momentous difcoveries that had been made in the heavens, by Copernicus, Tycho Brahe, Galileo, Kepler, and others, yet aftronomy, as Lord Bacon complained, ftill remained but a mathematical ftudy. The paffage to which I allude is long; but, as tending to illuftrate more than one particular relating to my fubject, I cannot forbear trefpaffing on your indulgence by the citation. ‘ Al-
‘ though aftronomy,’ fays Bacon, ‘ has

‘ not been founded amifs upon obfervation
‘ of the phænomena, yet the fuperftructure
‘ has hitherto kept low and weakly. In
‘ truth that fcience prefents to the human
‘ underftanding fuch an object as PROME-
‘ THEUS did of old to JUPITER, when,
‘ meaning to impofe upon that deity, he
‘ offered upon his altar, inftead of a live
‘ victim, the hide of a large bullock,
‘ ftuffed with ftraw, leaves, and ofier
‘ branches. In like manner, aftronomy
‘ exhibits the externals of the celeftial
‘ bodies, as the cuticular part of heaven,
‘ fair, indeed, and artificially formed into
‘ a fyftem; but the entrails and the foun-
‘ tains of life are wanting, that is, the
‘ phyfical caufes and reafons; from which,
‘ and from aftronomical hypothefes, a the-
‘ ory fhould be drawn, not adequate only
‘ to account for all the phænomena, but
‘ for the fubftance, the motion, and influx
‘ of the heavens, as they are in Nature.—

6   ‘ Scarcely

' Scarcely is there one to be found, who
' has enquired into the natural caufes,
' either of the fubftance of celeftial matter,
' or into the reafon of the fwiftnefs or
' flownefs of the heavenly bodies acting
' upon one another; or into the various
' degrees of motion of the fame planet, or
' into the motion from eaft to weft, or of
' the contrary direction; nor into the pro-
' greffions, ftations, and retrogradations of
' thofe bodies; nor into the caufes of the
' apogæum and perigæum.—I fay, inqui-
' ries of this kind have fcarcely been at-
' tempted, nor indeed any labour beftowed
' upon the fubject, excepting in the way
' of mathematical obfervations and demon-
' ftrations. So that aftronomy, fuch as it
' now is, can only be reckoned among the
' mathematical arts; not without confider-
' able diminution of its dignity, fince, were
' it to maintain its rights, it might rank
' itfelf as the nobleft branch of philofophy.

I 2   ' For

' For he that fhall rejeft the fiftitious di-
' vorces between the fuperlunary and fub-
' lunary bodies, and fhall duly attend to
' the appetences and moft general affeftions
' of matter (which both in the earth and
' in the heavens are exceedingly powerful,
' and indeed pervade the univerfe), will
' receive, from what he fees paffing on the
' earth, clear information concerning the
' nature of celeftial bodies ; and contrari-
' wife, from motions which he fhall difco-
' ver in the heavens, will learn many par-
' ticulars relating to the things below, that
' now lie concealed from us. Wherefore
' the phyfical part of aftronomy we mark
' as *wanting*, and call it the *aftronomia*
' *viva*, the animated aftronomy, in oppo-
' fition to the ftuffed bullock of PROME-
' THEUS*.'

THE great *defideratum* was fupplied, and
from the bofom of this Society, in the

* De Dign. & Augm. Scient. l. iii. c. 4.

publication

publication of the *Principia*, the immortal
work of NEWTON. There the illuftrious
author evinces truths that had been only
furmifed before ; and, after eftablifhing by
a juft analyfis the laws of attraction, in a
fynthetical method proceeds to explain by
them the motions and appearances of the
heavenly bodies. Had not NEWTON lived,
BACON might have paffed for a vifionary
fpeculator ; but fince the demands of that
noble author upon the human intellects
have been fo fully anfwered in the productions of Sir ISAAC NEWTON, fhall we not
revere thofe powers of his own mind, that
could, in that dawn of philofophy in which
he lived, fo well defcry what parts were
wanting, and what were the means of attaining them ?

NEWTON, in a pofthumous treatife, *de
Syftemate Mundi*, compofed before the

publication

publication of the *Principia*, and mentioned there, has faid, that ' fome of the latter ' philofophers had fought to account for ' the courfe of the planets in their orbits ' by the action of certain *vortices*, as KEP-' LER and DESCARTES ; or by fome other ' principle of impulfe or attraction, as Bo-' RELLI, HOOKE, and others of our na-' tion.' From this paffage it would feem that, in thofe times, there had been more conjectures formed concerning attraction, than what were publifhed ; for, excepting GILBERT, who vainly attempted to explain the mundane fyftem by magnetifm, and Lord BACON, who never acceded to the *Copernican* hypothefis*, I have found none of our nation, HOOKE excepted, who, in this way, have left any thing on record

* ' Atque harum fuppofitionum abfurditas, in mo-
' tum terræ diurnum, (*quod nobis conftat falfiffimum*
' *effe*) homines impegit.'—Bac. de Dign. & Augm.
Scient. lib. iii. cap. iv.

worthy

worthy of your notice. He, indeed, the early, the ingenious, and moſt uſeful member of this Society, advanced, in this reſearch, far beyond all that had gone befcre him. But I ſhall not enlarge upon his improvements, as you have in your hands his *Cutlerian Lectures*, which contain them, and as I have already but too long dwelt on this part of my ſubject. It will ever redound to the praiſe of HOOKE, that NEWTON has aſſociated him with himſelf in maintaining the true regulating cauſe of the courſe of the planets*. As to BoRELLI, though I have found in one of the pieces (a ſcarce one) of that learned Italian, a paſſage that certainly favours attraction; yet as it is neither ſo full nor ſo explicit, upon that point, as ſeveral others which I have cited, I muſt ſuſpect that thoſe parts,

---

* M. MONTUCLA has done great juſtice to Dr. HOOKE, in this and other particulars, in his excellent work, *Hiſt. de Mathem.* part iv. liv. 8,

I 4 which

which Sir IsAAC had in his eye, have
efcaped my obfervation *.

THE great completer of the doctrine of
univerfal gravitation had the fatisfaction to
find, from the reception it met with in this
Society, that he had not laboured in vain :
nay, perhaps no philofophical author was
ever more admired and followed, in his
own time and in his own country, than
NEWTON was in thefe kingdoms. With
regard to others, ' we are not to wonder,'

---

* This is the paffage alluded to : ' Præterea mani-
' feftum eft, quemlibet five primarium five fecunda-
' rium planetam aliquem infignem mundi globum,
' quafi virtutis fontem, circumdare, qui ita eos ftrin-
' git atque conglutinat, ut ab ipfo nullo pacto abftra-
' hi poffint; fed ipfum, quacunque contendentem,
' perpetuis continuifque orbibus cogantur confequi :
' videmus enim Saturnum, Jovem, Martem, Vene-
' rem, atque Mercurium, Solem ipfum,—Medicæa
' Sidera, Jovem,—Hugenianumque Sidus, Saturnum
' circumire, non fecus, ac circa Telluris Globum
' Luna ipfa revolvitur.'—Joa. Alph. Borelli Theor.
Medic. Planetar. ex Caufis Phyficis deductæ, lib. i.
cap. ii. p. 5. Florent. 1666, 4to,

as remarked by his eloquent Eulogift, ' if
' philofophers, upon the firft publication
' of the *Principia*, took the alarm at the
' term *attraction*, as fearing the return of
' the *occult qualities*; or if, confidering the
' difficulty of the fubject, and the few
' words employed in explaining it, they
' wanted time fully to comprehend it *.'
Thefe obftacles have been removing by
degrees, and the way at laft has been fo
effectually cleared, that the name of NEW-
TON is not perhaps held in more eftimation here, nor his principles more cordially
embraced, than in thofe very focieties of
the learned abroad, which at firft fhewed
moft unbelief, and at whofe converfion,
therefore, we ought moft to rejoice.

THE Royal Academy of Sciences, whilft
in an uncertain ftate between the old and
new fyftem of philofophy, having, for one

* Eloge de Newton, par M. de Fontenelle.

of

of the decifive experiments, meafured fome
degrees of latitude upon an arch of a meridian pafling through Paris, and compared
this menfuration with others, inferred the
earth to be a fpheroid, with the longeft
diameter pafling through its poles; but,
fenfible that this operation had not been fo
unexceptionably conducted as to fatisfy either the followers of NEWTON or thofe of
HUYGENS, who both required a fpheroid
flattened at the poles, refolved upon a farther and more accurate trial. With this
view, in the year 1735, fome chofen
members from that illuftrious Body were
fent to the polar circle, and others to the
equator; at which places the differences of
degrees being greater, the point in difpute
might be determined with lefs danger of
error. How much to the honour of NEW-
TON and HUYGENS the refult was, is fufficiently known. All that is neceffary to
be mentioned here, is, that, in the year

1738,

1738, whilft the academicians were ftill in
Peru, it cccurred to M. BOUGUER, one of
that number, to put the *Newtonian* fyftem
to another teft, by enquiring into the attraction of mountains. This idea, which
was originally from NEWTON himfelf, M.
BOUGUER communicated to his colleague
M. DE LA CONDAMINE, who readily affifted in making the trial *. Thofe gentlemen were perfuaded, that if the whole
mafs of the earth were really poffeffed of
fuch a property, a high mountain, fuch as
Nature had abundantly provided in that
country, would fhew fome proportionable
degree of it ; and that the largeft of the
Andes was indeed but a fmall object in
comparifon of the earth : neverthelefs they
reekoned, by a rough computation, that
the attraction of Chimboraço, which they
deemed the beft for their purpofe, would

* BOUGUER, Figure de la Terre, fect. 7. DE LA
CONDAMINE, 'Journal du Voyage à l' Equateur.

be

be equal to about the 2000th part of the attraction of the whole earth. Now, here the mountain acting as one, whilst the earth acted as 2000, the direction of gravity would be vifibly turned out of the vertical line, for as much as this direction would be 1' and 43" towards the mountain. But how was this deflexion to be eftimated? Only by finding the quantity of deviation of the plumb-line from a vertical pofition, by means of ftars. In order to attain this point, they found it moft convenient, in their prefent circumftances, to take the diftance of feveral ftars from the zenith, at two ftations, one on the fouth fide of Chimboraço, and the other a league and a half to the weft; that is, at fuch a diftance from the firft ftation, as that the plumb-line fhould be but little affected by the mountain. This difpofition being made, they proceeded to their operations, of which we have a full and clear account by M.

BOUGUER,

BOUGUER, in his valuable treatife entitled *Figure de la Terre ;* but of M. DE LA CONDAMINE, we have only a fhort ab-ftract of the narrative he prefented to the Academy ; which abftract is contained in his curious *Journal of a Voyage to the Equator.*

FROM both it appears, that though thefe learned perfons, during the time employed in this experiment (which the inclemency of the air, at that height in the atmofphere, forced them to make very fhort),—I fay, though during this time they fpared no pains, yet their obfervations not only va-ried from one another, but feemed to be little fatisfactory to themfelves. M. BOU-GUER fays, that, inftead of 1′ 43″, which the plumb-line ought to have declined from the true vertical line, the total de-clenfion amounted only to feven feconds and a half: an effect that fell far fhort of the

expecta-

expectations of a *Newtonian*. But thofe
candid gentlemen take notice, that, ' as on
' one hand we are ignorant of the denfity
' of the internal parts of the earth, which
' may be confiderably greater than what
' appears by its furface; fo, on the other,
' Chimboraço, which they believed likely
' to be as folid as any other parts of the
' furface of the earth, might neverthelefs,
' in many places, be hollow.' Nay, M.
DE LA CONDAMINE tells us, that ' he was
' afterwards informed of a tradition in the
' country, that this very monntain had
' once been a volcano;' and adds, that
' whilft he and his colleague were about
' their experiment, they had actually found
' fome calcined ftones upon it:' from which
circumftances he infers, that ' if one cannot
' juft draw from this trial an abfolute proof
' of the *Newtonian* attraction, one can far
' lefs form any conclufion againft it.' M.
BOUGUER goes farther, and obferves, that
' if

' if we will be fatisfied with the bare fact,
' it is certain, from this experiment, that
' mountains do act at a diftance, but that
' their action is much lefs than what might
' be expected from their bulk.' He con-
cludes his account in the true fpirit of a
philofopher, by faying, that ' as in France,
' or in England, a hill may be found of a
' fufficient height for the purpofe, and
' efpecially if the obferver would double
' the action, by making a ftation on each
' fide ; he fhould be happy to hear, on his
' return to Europe, that the experiment
' had been repeated, whether the refult
' tended to confirm his obfervations, or to
' throw fome better light upon that en-
' quiry.' If the Society have fulfilled the
views of that worthy man, who thus called
upon them, we have to regret that he did
not live long enough to fhare the fatisfaction with us.

I COME

I COME now to Mr. MASKELYNE's labours, upon which I fhall not expatiate, as
I have already taken up too much of your
time, and as I judge it unneceffary to dwell
long upon that part of my fubject, which
you have fo lately heard in his own words,
and which you will have in a few days
publifhed at large in your Tranfactions.

I NEED only remind you, that the zenith diftance of a ftar on the meridian being obferved at two ftations under the fame
meridian, one on the fouth fide of a mountain, the other on the north; if the plumb-
line of the inftrument be attracted by the
mountain out of its vertical pofition, the
ftar will appear too much to the north, by
the obfervation at the fouthern ftation, and
too much to the fouth, by that at the
northern ftation; and confequently the
difference of the latitudes of the two ftations will be found, by thefe obfervations,

greater

greater than it really is. And if the true difference of their latitudes be determined by meafuring the diftance between the two ftations on the ground, the excefs of the difference, found by the obfervations of the ftar, above that found by this meafurement, muft have been produced by the attraction of the mountain, and its half will be the effect of fuch attraction on the plumb-line at each obfervation, fuppofing the mountain attracts equally on both fides.

To perform this experiment, Mr. MAS-KELYNE made choice of the mountain Schehallien, in Perthfhire in North Britain, of which the direction in length is nearly eaft and weft; its height above the furrounding valley, at a medium, is about 2000 feet; and its higheft part, above the level of the fea, is 3550 feet. As the greateft attraction of the mountain was to

K   be

be expected about half way up its fides
(which happened, conveniently for the
purpofe of the experiment, to be pretty
fteep), two ftations for an obfervatory were
accordingly chofen, one on the north, the
other on the fouth fide of Schehallien.
The inftrument, with which he obferved
the ftars, was an excellent fector made by
Mr. SISSON; and Mr. MASKELYNE has
related at large all the precautions he took
both for adjufting this inftrument in the
meridian at each ftation, and for fatisfying
himfelf that the line of collimation remained unaltered. From obfervations of ten
ftars near the zenith, he found the apparent difference of the latitudes of the two
ftations to be 54″, 6; and from a meafurement by triangles, formed from two bafes
on different fides of the mountain, he found
the diftance of their parallels to be 4364
feet, which, in the latitude of Schehallien,
viz. 56° 40′, anfwer to an arch of the me-

4   ridian

ridian of $43''$: this is $11''$, 6 lefs than that found by the fector. Its half, therefore, $5''$, 8, is the mean effect of the attraction of the mountain : and from its magnitude, compared with the bulk of the whole earth, Mr. MASKELYNE difcovered the mean denfity of the earth to be about double that of the mountain.

IN the execution of this interefting experiment, our worthy brother has not only exerted a patience and perfeverance, but a fagacity and judgment, which muft ever redound to his honour. All doubts about an univerfal attraction muft at laft be terminated, and every philofopher, in that refpect, muft now become a *New-tonian.*

IF I have related but two experiments that have been made, the firft by the French academicians, and the other by

Mr.

Mr. MASKELYNE, it is becaufe no more have come to our knowledge; nor do I believe that more have actually been executed. For if, in occafional menfurations of degrees of the meridian in different parts of Europe, thofe employed have found varieties arife in their meafures, that they could not otherwife account for, than from the attraction of the mountains among which they carried on their operations, and accordingly have referred thofe irregularities to that very caufe; fuch conjectures we admit may be well founded, but the meafurements whence they arife we cannot reckon among the experiments we now treat of.

BUT was not the doctrine of an univerfal attraction fo fully demonftrated by NEWTON, as not to require any farther proofs from experiments? Demonftrated it was, but not to the conviction of every

8   individual.

individual. True Philofophy condefcends to adapt her inftructions to different capacities, and is as willing to inform by palpable experiments as by geometrical demonftrations. But to fay the truth, fomething feemed wanting here for the fatisfaction of even the more enlightened minds. Such we reckon thofe were, who firft made the trial. And did not HUYGENS himfelf, one of the greateft philofophers and geometricians of his age, find difficulties about this principle, even after the publication of NEWTON's *Principia?* Nor do we learn that the doubts of that great man were ever removed *. To fay nothing of the celebrated LEIBNITZ, and his numerous followers, who to this day are either wholly unbelievers in attraction, or at beft but fceptics on that article.

You have, therefore, GENTLEMEN, the fatisfaction to think that you have com-

* Vid. Huygen. Differt. de Cauf. Gravitat.

pletcd

pleted a great and acceptable work to the
fcientific world ; and that, though this has
been a coftly experiment, your gracious
PATRON, who fo liberally furnifhed the
means, will highly approve your expend-
ing his benefaction fo much for the advancement of Natural Knowledge and for
the benefit of the Public ; and will fo much
the more be difpofed to fhew you the like
favour on future occafions.

BUT even thofe who wanted no frefh
proofs of the univerfality of attraction,
muft ftill partake of the advantages accruing from this experiment, as being
not only the firft that has been made, but
the beft that could be devifed, for eftimat-
ing the mean denfity of the earth. The
operation in Peru was too imperfect for
that purpofe ; and had the circumftances of
that trial been more favourable, yet the
fufpicion of the mountain's having been

once

once a volcano, was a fufficient reafon for
admitting no evidence from it in this part
of our inquiry. But for Schehallien, as its
appearance was particularly rocky, and as
feveral fpecimens of its rocks have been
prefented to the Society, and acknowledged
to be mineral fubftances that had never
paffed through fire, we may confider that
mountain as one of the proper patterns
of the denfity of the furface of the earth.

THESE, GENTLEMEN, are the fruits of
the operations of Mr. MASKELYNE, during
a refidence of four months in a mean hut,
on the fide of a bleak mountain, and in a
climate little favourable to celeftial obfervations. To thefe inconveniences, however,
he fubmitted with patience and compla-
cency, as he went at your requeft, and in
purfuit of fcience. You have heard his
chief conclufions ; but permit me add,
that, as this is a new mine opened in the

field

field of Nature, I am confident that thefe
will not be the only productions; but that,
as in all great and fuccefsful experiments,
there will be, in the profecution of this
fubject, fome valuable truths brought to
light, of which at prefent we can form no
particular conjecture. Mean while we have
the pleafure to find the doctrine of *univerfal gravitation* fo firmly eftablifh_d by this
finifhing ftep of analyfis, that the moft
fcrupulous now can no longer hefitate to
embrace a principle, that gives life to Aftronomy, by accounting for the various motions and appearances of the Hofts of
Heaven.

MR. MASKELYNE,

THE judgment, SIR, of the Council,
in awarding you the Prize, having received

the

the fanction of the Royal Society, I do, in
the name and by the authority of that
illuftrious Body, prefent you, their moft
worthy Brother, with this fincere pledge
of their affection ; as the lafting token of
their acknowledgment for your feveral ingenious and ufeful communications, and
more particularly for this laft painful and
capital experiment, which adds no fmall
luftre to their Tranfactions. And after
expreffing their grateful fentiments for
what you have already done for their
fervice, I would farther fay, that they
perfuade themfelves, from your talents,
your love of your profeffion, and your
happy period of life, you will continue
fteadily to purfue that path which you
have fo early entered upon, and which
fo furely leads to great and ufeful difcoveries. You have, SIR, in charge the
nobleft branch of Natural Philofophy :
fuch it has ever been held by this Society,

and

and as fuch it ever has been cherifhed
and cultivated by them. And they flatter themfelves that their cares and folicitude have not been fruitlefs; fince, from
their firft inftitution to this day, there
have never been wanting fome excellent
men in that line, to promote the fcience,
and do honour to this Community. But
fo tranfcendently great is that part of the
creation, that though the Divine Author
has vouchfafed, in thefe latter days, to
open, to the humble and patient inquirers
into Nature, the *Caufes of Things;* yet
we muft ftill cry with the ancient fage,
*Lo, thefe are part of His ways, but how
little a portion is heard of them!* As
much then remains to be explored in
the celeftial regions, you are encouraged,
SIR, by what has been already attained,
to perfevere in thefe hallowed labours,
from which have been derived the greateft improvements in the moft ufeful arts,

and

and the loudeſt declaràtions of the power,
the wiſdom, and the goodneſs of the Supreme Architect, in the ſpacious and beautiful fabric of the World.

A

DISCOURSE

UPON

SOME LATE IMPROVEMENTS

OF THE MEANS FOR

PRESERVING the HEALTH of MARINERS;

DELIVERED AT THE

Anniverſary Meeting of the ROYAL SOCIETY,

November 30, 1775.

By Sir JOHN PRINGLE, Bart. PRESIDENT.

PUBLISHED BY THEIR ORDER.

A

DISCOURSE

UPON

SOME LATE IMPROVEMENTS

OF THE MEANS FOR

PRESERVING THE HEALTH OF MARINERS.

GENTLEMEN,

BEFORE we proceed farther in the bufinefs of this day, permit me to acquaint you with the judgment of your Council in the difpofal of Sir GODFREY COPLEY's Medal; an office I have under-taken at their requeft, and with the greater fatisfaction, as I am confident you will be

no

lefs unanimous in giving your approbation, than they have been in addreffing you for it upon this occafion. For though they were not infenfible of the juft title that feveral of the Papers, compofing the prefent volume of your Tranfactions, had to your particular notice, yet they did not hefitate in preferring that which I prefented to you from Captain COOK, giving *An Account of the Method he had taken to preferve the Health of the Crew of his Majefty's Ship, the* Refolution, *during her late Voyage round the World.* Indeed, I imagine that the name alone of fo worthy a Member of this Society would have inclined you to depart from the ftrictnefs of your rules, by conferring upon him that honour, though you had received no direct communication from him; confidering how meritorious in your eyes that perfon muft appear, who hath not only made the moft extenfive, but the moft inftructive voyages;

ages; who hath not only difcovered, but furveyed, vaft tracts of new coafts; who hath difpelled the illufion of a *terra auftralis incognita*, and fixed the bounds of the habitable earth, as well as thofe of the navigable ocean, in the fouthern hemifphere.

I SHALL not, however, expatiate on that ample field of praife, but confine my difcourfe to what was the intention of this honorary premium, namely, to crown that Paper of the year, which fhould contain the moft ufeful and moft fuccefsful experimental enquiry. Now what enquiry can be fo ufeful as that, which hath for its object the faving the lives of men? And when fhall we find one more fuccefsful than that before us? Here are no vain boaftings of the empiric, nor ingenious and delufive theories of the dogmatift; but a concife, and artlefs, and an inconteſted relation of the means, by which, ' under the

L   ' divine

' divine favour, Captain COOK, with a
' company of an hundred and eighteen
' men*, performed a voyage of three years
' and eighteen days, throughout all the
' climates, from fifty-two degrees north to
' seventy-one degrees south, with the lofs
' of only one man by ficknefs †.' What
muft enhance to us the value of thefe falutary obfervations, is, to fee that the practice
hath been no lefs fimple than efficacious.

I WOULD now enquire of the moft con-
verfant in the ftudy of bills of mortality,
whether, in the moft healthful climate, and

---

* There were on board, in all, one hundred and
eighteen men, including M. Sparrman and his fer-
vant, but whom they took in at the Cape of Good
Hope, and left there upon their return to that place.

† This was a confumption terminating in a dropfy.
Mr. Patten, furgeon to the Refolution, who mentioned to me this cafe, obferved that this man began
fo early to complain of a cough and other confumptive
fymptoms, which had never left him, that his lungs
muft have been affected before he came on board.

in

in the beft condition of life, they have ever
found fo fmall a number of deaths, in fuch
a number of men, within that fpace of
time? How great and agreeable then muft
our furprife be, after perufing the hiftories
of long navigations in former days, when
fo many perifhed by marine difeafes, to
find the air of the fea acquitted of all ma-
lignity, and, in fine, that a voyage round
the world may be undertaken with lefs
danger, perhaps, to health, than a common
tour in Europe!

BUT the better to fee the contraft between the old and the prefent times, allow
me to recal to your memory what you
have read of the firft voyage for the eftablifhment of the Eaft India Company*.
The equipment confifting of four fhips,

* This fquadron, under the command of LANCAS-
TER (who was called the General), fet out in the
year 1601. See PURCHAS's Pilgr. vol. i. p. 147,
& feq.

with

with four hundred and eighty men on
board, three of thefe veffels were fo weakened by the fcurvy, by the time they had
got only three degrees beyond the Line,
that the merchants, who had embarked on
this adventure, were obliged to do duty as
common failors ; and there died, in all, at
fea, and on fhore at Soldania, a place of
refrefhment on this fide the Cape of Good
Hope, one hundred and five men, which
was nearly a fourth part of their comple-
ment, before they got farther on their
voyage. And hath not Sir RICHARD
HAWKINS, who lived in that age, an intelligent as well as brave officer, recorded,
that ' in twenty years, during which he
' had ufed the fea, he could give an ac-
' count of ten thoufand mariners, who had
' been confumed by the fcurvy alone * ?'
Yet fo far was this author from miftaking
the difeafe, that I have perufed few who

* PURCHAS's Pilgr. vol. iv. p. 1373, & feq.

have

have fo well defcribed it. If, then, in thofe early times, the infancy, I may call them, of the commerce and naval power of England, fo many were carried off by that bane of fea-faring people, what muft have been the deftruction afterwards, upon the great augmentation of the fleet, and the opening of fo many new ports to the trade of this country, whilft fuch little advancement was made in the nautical part of medicine!

But paffing from thefe old dates to one within the remembrance of many here prefent, when it might have been expected that whatever tended to aggrandize the naval power of Great Britain, and to extend her commerce, would have received the higheft improvement; yet we fhall find that, even at that late period, few meafures had been taken to preferve the health of feamen, more than had been known to our

uninftructed

uninftructed anceftors. Of this affertion, the victorious but mournful expedition of Commodore ANSON affords too convincing a proof. It is well known that, foon after paffing the Straits of Le Maire, the fcurvy began to appear in his fquadron; that, by the time the Centurion had advanced but a little way into the South Sea, forty-feven had died of it in that fhip; and that there were few on board who had not, in fome degree, been affected with the diftemper, though they had not been quite eight months from England: that, in the ninth month, when ftanding for the ifland of Juan Fernandez, the Centurion loft double that number; and that the mortality went on at fo great a rate (I ftill fpeak of the Commodore's fhip) that, before they arrived there, fhe had buried two hundred; and at laft could mufter no more than two quarter-mafters and fix of the foremaft-men, in a watch, capable of doing duty.

This

This was the condition of one of the three ſhips which reached that iſland; the other two ſuffered in proportion.

Nor did the tragedy end here: for after a few months reſpite, the ſame fatal ſick-neſs broke out afreſh, and made ſuch ha-vock, that, before the Centurion (which now contained the whole ſurviving crew of the three ſhips) had got to the iſland of Tinian, there died ſometimes eight or ten in a day; infomuch that, when they had been only two years on their voyage, they had loſt a larger proportion than of four in five of their original number; and, by the account of the hiſtorian, all of them, after their entering the South Sea, of the ſcurvy. I ſay, by the account of the elegant writer of that voyage; for, as he neither was in the medical line himſelf, nor hath authen-ticated this part of his narrative by appeal-ing to the ſurgeons of the ſhip, or to their

journals,

journals, I fhould doubt that this was not
ftrictly the cafe; but rather that, in producing this great mortality, a peftilential
kind of diftemper was joined to the fcurvy,
which, from the places where it moft frequently occurs, hath been diftinguifhed by
the name of *the jail* or *hofpital fever**. But
whether the fcurvy alone, or this fever
combined with it, were the caufe, it is not
at prefent material to enquire; fince both,
arifing from foul air and other fources of
putrefaction, may now in a great meafure
be obviated by the various means fallen
upon fince Lord ANSON's expedition. For,
in juftice to that prudent as well as brave
Commander, it muft be obferved, that the
arrangements, preparatory to his voyage,
were not made by himfelf; that his fhip

---

* Dr. MEAD, who had feen the original obfervations of two of Commodore ANSON's furgeons, fays,
that the fcurvy, at that time, was accompanied with
putrid fevers, &c. See his Treatife on the Scurvy,
p. 98, & feq.

was

was fo deeply laden, as not, except in the calmeft weather, to admit of opening the gun-ports for the benefit of air; and that nothing appears to have been neglected by him, for preferving the health of his men, that was then known and practifed in the navy.

I SHOULD now proceed to enumerate the chief improvements made fince that time, and which have enabled our fhips to make fo many fuccefsful circumnavigations, as in a manner to efface the impref-fion of former difafters; but as I have mentioned the ficknefs moft deftructive to failors, and againft the ravages of which thofe prefervatives have been mainly con-trived, it may be proper briefly to explain its nature, and the rather as, excepting among mariners, it is little underftood. Firft, then, I would obferve, that the fcurvy is not the difeafe which goes by

that

that name on fhore. The diftemper commonly, but erroneoufly, in this country,
called the *fcurvy*, belongs to a clafs of difeafes totally different from what we are
now treating of; and fo far is the common
received opinion, that *that there are few
conftitutions altogether free from a fcorbutic
taint*, from being true, that, unlefs among
failors and others circumftanced like them,
more particularly with refpect to thofe who
ufe a falt and putrid diet, and efpecially if
they live in foul air and uncleanlinefs, I
have reafon to believe there are few diforders lefs frequent. This opinion I fubmitted to the judgment of the Society feveral
years ago, and I have had no reafon fince
to alter it. I then faid, contrary to what
was generally believed, but feemingly on
the beft grounds, that the fea-air was never
the caufe of the fcurvy, fince, on board a
fhip on the longeft voyages, cleanlinefs,
ventilation, and frefh provifions, would
preferve

preferve from it; and that upon a fea-
coaft, free from marfhes, the inhabitants
were not liable to that indifpofition, though
frequently breathing the air from the fea *.
I concluded with joining in fentiment with
thofe, who afcribed the fcurvy to a feptic
refolution, that is, a beginning corruption
of the whole habit, fimilar to that of every
animal fubftance when deprived of life †.
This account feemed to be fufficiently verified by the examination of the fymptoms
in the fcorbutic fick, and by the appearances in their bodies after death ‡. On
that occafion I remarked, that falted meats,
after fome time, become in reality putrid,
though they may contiue long palatable by.

* Difeafes of the Army, part i. ch. 2. Append
Pap. 7.

† Ibid.

‡ WOODALL's Surgeon's Mate, p. 163. POU-
PART. Mem. de l' Acad. R. des Sc. A. 1699. PETIT,
Mal. des Os, tom. ii. p. 446. MEAD on the Scurvy,
p. 104.

means

means of the falt; and that common falt, fuppofed to be one of the ftrongeft prefervatives from corruption, is at beft but an indifferent one, even in a large quantity; and in a fmall one, fuch as we ufe at table with frefh meats, or fwallow in meats that have been falted, fo far from impeding putrefaction, it rather promotes that procefs in the body.

THIS pofition concerning the putrefying quality of fea-falt, in certain proportions, hath been fince confirmed by the experiments of the late Mr. CANTON, Fellow of this Society, in a Paper on the *Caufe of the Luminous Appearance of Sea-Water**.

IT hath been alleged, that the fcurvy is much owing to the coldnefs of the air, which checks perfpiration, and on that account is the endemic diftemper of the

* Phil. Tranfact. vol. lix. p. 446.

northern

northern nations, particularly of thofe around the Baltic *. The fact is partly true, but, I doubt, not fo the caufe. In thofe regions, by the long and fevere win- ters, the cattle, deftitute of pafture, can barely live, and are therefore unfit for ufe; fo that the people, for their provifion dur- ing that feafon, are obliged to flaughter them by the end of autumn, and to falt them for above half the year. This putrid diet, then, on which they muft fo long fubfift, and to which the inhabitants of the South are not reduced, feems to be the chief caufe of the difeafe. And if we reflect that the lower people of the North have few or no greens nor fruit in the winter, little or no fermented liquors, and often live in damp, foul, and ill-aired houfes, it is eafy to con- ceive how they fhould become liable to the fame diforder with feamen; whilft others,

* BARTHOLIN. Med. Danor. Domeftic. p. 98.

of

of as high a latitude, but who live in a different manner, keep free from it. Thus we are informed, by LINNÆUS, that the Laplanders, one of the moſt hyperborean nations, know nothing of the ſcurvy*; for which no other reaſon can be aſſigned than their never eating putrid and ſalted meats, nor indeed ſalt with any thing, but their uſing all the winter the freſh fleſh of their rein-deer.

THIS exemption of the Laplanders from the general diſtemper of the North, is the more obſervable, as they ſeldom taſte vegetables, bread never, as we farther learn from that celebrated author. Yet, in the very provinces which border on Lapland, where they uſe bread, but ſcarcely any other vegetable, and eat ſalted meats, they are as much troubled with the ſcurvy as in

* LINNÆI Flora Lapponica, p. 8, 9.

any

any other country *. But let us incident-
ally remark, that the late improvements in
agriculture, gardening, and in the other
arts of life, by extending their influence to
the remoteſt parts of Europe, and to the
loweſt people, begin fenfibly to leffen the
frequency of that complaint, even in thoſe
climates that have been once the moſt afflicted with it.

It hath alfo been afferted, that men living on ſhore will be affected with the fcurvy, though they have never been confined
to falted meats ; but of this I have known
no inſtance, except in thoſe who breathed
a marſhy air, or what was otherwiſe putrid, and who wanted exercife, fruits, and
the common herbs : under fuch circumftances, it muſt be owned that the humours .

* LINNÆUS, in feveral parts of his work, confirms
what is here faid of falted meats, as one of the chief
caufes of the fcurvy. See Amœnitat. Acad. vol. v.
p. 6. & feq. p. 42.

will

will corrupt in the fame manner, though
not in the fame degree, with thofe of feamen. Thus, in the late war, when Sifing-
hurft Caftle in Kent was filled with French
prifoners, the fcurvy broke out among
them, notwithftanding they had never been
ferved with falted victuals in England, but
had daily had an allowance of frefh meat,
and of bread in proportion, though without
greens or other vegetables. The country
furgeon who attended them, and from
whom I received this information, having
formerly been employed in the navy, was
the better able to judge of the diforder, and
to cure it. Befides the deficiency of herbs,
he obferved that the wards were foul and
crowded, the houfe damp (from a moat
that furrounded it), and that the bounds
allotted for taking the air were fo fmall,
and in wet weather fo floughy, that the
men feldom cared to go out. He added,
that a reprefentation having been made, he

had

had been empowered to furnifh the prifoners with roots and greens for boiling in
their foup, and to quarter the fick in a
neighbouring village, in a dry fituation,
with liberty to go out for air and exercife ;
and that by thefe means they had all quickly recovered. It is probable, that the
fcurvy fooner appeared among thefe ftrangers, from their having been taken at fea,
and being, from their diet, more difpofed
to the difeafe. My informer farther acquainted me, that, in the lower and wetter
parts of that county, where fome of his
practice lay, he had now and then met
with flighter cafes of the fcurvy among the
common people ; fuch, he faid, as lived
the whole winter on falted bacon, without
fermented liquors, greens, or fruit, a few
apples excepted ; but he remarked, that,
in the winters following a plentiful growth
of apples, thefe peafants were manifeftly
lefs liable to the complaint.

M   I HAVE

I HAVE dwelt the longer on this part of
my fubject, as I look upon the knowledge of
the nature and caufe of the fcurvy to be an
effential ftep towards improving the means
of prevention and cure. And I am perfuaded, after mature reflection, and the
opportunities I have had of converfing with
thofe, who to much fagacity had joined no
fmall experience in nautical practice, that,
upon an examination of the feveral articles,
which have either been of old approved, or
have of late been introduced into the navy,
it will be found, that, though thefe means
may vary in form, and in their mode of
operating; yet that they all fome way contribute towards preventing or correcting
putrefaction, whether of the air in the clofer
parts of a fhip, of the meats, of the water,
of the clothes and bedding, or of the body
itfelf. And, if in this inquiry (which may
be made by the way, whilft we take a review of the principal articles of provifion,

and

and other methods ufed by Captain Cook
to guard againft the fcurvy), I fay, if in
this inquiry it fhall appear, that the notion
of a feptic or putrid origin, is not without
foundation, it will be no fmall encouragement to proceed on that principle, in order
farther to improve this important branch of
medicine.

Captain Cook begins his lift of his
prefervative ftores with *malt :* ' Of this,' he
fays, ' was made *fweet wort*, and given not
' only to thofe men who had manifeft
' fymptoms of the fcurvy, but to fuch alfo
' as were judged to be moft liable to it.'
Dr. Macbride, who firft fuggefted this
preparation, was led (as he obferves) to the
difcovery by fome experiments that had
been laid before this Society, by which it
appeared that the air produced by aliment-
ary fermentation was endowed with a

M 2   power

power of correcting putrefaction *. The fact he confirmed by numerous trials; and, finding this fluid to be the *fixed air*, he juftly concluded, that whatever fubftance, proper for food, abounded with it, and which could be conveniently carried to fea, would make one of the fureft remedies againft the fcurvy; which he then confidered as a *putrid difeafe*, and, as fuch, to be prevented or cured by that powerful kind of antifeptic †. Beer, for inftance, had always been efteemed one of the beft antifcorbutics; but, as that derived all its *fixed air* from the malt of which it was made, he inferred that malt itfelf was preferable in long voyages, as it took up lefs room than the brewed liquor, and would keep longer found. Experience hath fince verified this

---

* Append. to my *Obfervations on the Difeafes of the Army*.

* Macbride's Exper. Eff. *paffim*.

ingenious

ngenious theory; and the malt hath now
gained fo much credit in the navy, that
there only wanted fo long, fo healthful,
and fo celebrated a voyage as this, to rank
it among the moft indifpenfable articles of
provifion. For though Captain COOK remarks, that ' a proper attention to other
' things muft be joined, and that he is not
' altogether of opinion that the wort will
' be able to cure the fcurvy, in an advanced
' ftate, at fea ; yet he is perfuaded that it
' is fufficient to prevent that diftemper
' from making any great progrefs, for a
' confiderable time ;' and therefore he doth
not hefitate to pronounce it ' one of the
' beft antifcorbutic medicines yet found
' out *.'

THIS

* Having been favoured with a fight of the medical
journal of Mr. PATTEN, furgeon to the Refolution, I
read the following paffage in it, not a little ftrength-
ening the above teftimony : ' I have found the *wort*
' of the utmoft fervice, in all fcorbutic cafes, during

M 3   ' the

THIS falutary *gas* (or *fixed air*) is contained, more or lefs, in all fermentable
liquors, and begins to oppofe putrefaction,
as foon as the working or inteftine motion
commences.

IN wine, it abounds; and perhaps no
vegetable fubftance is more replete with it
than the juice of the grape. If we join
the grateful tafte of wine, we muft rank it
the firft in the lift of antifcorbutic liquors.
Cyder is likewife excellent, with other vi-
nous productions from fruit; as alfo the

' the voyage. As many took it by way of preven-
' tion, few cafes occurred where it had a fair trial;
' but thefe, however, I flatter myfelf, will be fuffi-
' cient to convince every impartial perfon, that it is
' the beft remedy hitherto found out for the cure of
' the fea-fcurvy: and I am well convinced, from
' what I have feen the *wort* perform, and from its
', mode of operation, that, if aided by *portable foup*,
' *four krout*, *fugar*, *fago*, and *courants*, the fcurvy,
' that maritime peftilence, will feldom or never make
' its alarming appearance among a fhip's crew, on the
' longeft voyages; proper care with regard to clean-
' linefs and provifions being obferved.'

various

various kinds of beer. It hath been a conftant obfervation, that, in long cruifes or
diftant voyages, the fcurvy is never feen
whilft the fmall-beer holds out at a full
allowance; but that, when it is all ex-
pended, the diftemper foon prevails. It
were therefore to be wifhed, that this moft·
wholefome beverage could be renewed at
fea; but our fhips afford not fufficient con-
venience. The Ruffians, however, make a
fhift to prepare on board, as well as at land,
fomething of a middle quality between
wort and fmall-beer, in the following manner: They take ground malt and rye-
meal, in a certain proportion, which they
knead into fmall loaves, and bake in the
oven. Thefe they occafionally infufe in a
proper quantity of warm water, which begins fo foon to ferment, that, in the fpace·
of twenty-four hours, their brewage is
completed, in the production of a fmall,
brifk, and acidulous liquor, they call *quas*,

palatable

palatable to themfelves, and not difagreeable to the tafte of ftrangers. The late Dr. MOUNSEY, fellow of this Society, who had lived long in Ruffia, and had been *Archiater* under two fucceffive fovereigns, acquainted me, that the *quas* was the common and falutary drink both of the fleets and armies of that empire, and that it was particularly good againft the fcurvy. He added, that, happening to be at Mofcow when he perufed my *Obfervations on the Jail and Hofpital Fever*, then lately publifhed *, he had been induced to compare what he read in that treatife with what he fhould fee in the feveral prifons of that large city. But, to his furprife, after vifiting them all, and finding them full of malefactors (for the late Emprefs at that time. fuffered none who were convicted of capi-

---

* That treatife was firft publifhed by itfelf, and afterwards incorporated with the *Obfervations on the Difeafes of the Army.*

tal

tal crimes to be put to death), he could difcover no fever among them, nor learn that any acute diftemper, peculiar to jails, had ever been known there. He obferved, that fome of thefe places of confinement had a yard, into which the prifoners were allowed to come for the air; but that there were others without that advantage, yet not fickly. So that he could affign no other reafon for the healthful condition of thefe men than the kind of diet they ufed, which was the fame with that of the common people of the country; who, not being able to purchafe flefh-meat, live moftly on rye-bread (the moft acefcent of any bread), and drink *quas*. He concluded with faying, that, upon his return to St. Peterfburg, he had made the fame enquiry there, and with the fame refult.

THUS far Dr. MOUNSEY; from whofe account it would feem, that the rye-meal

affifted

affifted both in quickening the fermentation
and adding more fixed air, fince the malt
alone could not fo readily produce fo tart
and brifk a liquor. And there is little
doubt, but that, whenever the other grains
can be brought to a proper degree of fermentation, they will, more or lefs, in the
fame way, become ufeful. That oats will,
I am fatisfied, from what I have been told
by one of the intelligent friends of Captain
Cook. This gentleman being on a cruize
in a large fhip *, in the beginning of the
late war, and the fcurvy breaking out
among his crew, he bethought himfelf of a
kind of food he had feen ufed in fome parts
of the country, as the moft proper on that
occafion. Some oat-meal is put into a
wooden veffel, hot water is poured upon
it, and the infufion continues until the
liquor begins to tafte fourifh, that is, till a
fermentation comes on, which, in a place

---

* The Effex, a feventy gun fhip.

moderately

moderately warm, may be in the ſpace of two days. The water is then poured off from the grounds, and boiled down to the conſiſtence of a jelly *. This he ordered to be made and dealt out in meſſes, being firſt ſweetened with ſugar, and ſeaſoned with ſome prize French wine, which, though turned ſour, yet improved the taſte, and made this aliment not leſs palatable than medicinal.

He aſſured me, that, upon this diet chiefly, and by abſtaining from ſalted meats, his *ſcorbutic* ſick had quite recovered on board ; and not in that voyage only, but, by the ſame means, in his ſubſequent cruizes during the war, without his being obliged to ſend one of them on ſhore be‑ cauſe they could not get well at ſea. Yet oat-meal unfermented, like barley unmalt- ed, hath no ſenſible effect in curing the

* This rural food, in the North, is called *ſooins*.

ſcurvy;

fcurvy ; as if the *fixed air*, which is incorporated with thefe grains, could mix with
the chyle which they produce, enter the
lacteals with it, and make part of the nourifhment of the body, without manifefting
any elaftic or antifeptic quality, when not
loofened by a previous fermentation.

BEFORE the power of the *fixed air*, in
fubduing putrefaction, was known, the efficacy of fruits, greens, and fermented liquors, was commonly afcribed to the acid
in their compofition ; and we have ftill
reafon to believe that the acid concurs in
producing that effect. If it be alleged that
mineral acids, which contain little or no
fixed air, have been ufed in the fcurvy with
little fuccefs ; I would anfwer, that I doubt
that, in thofe trials, they have never·been
fufficiently diluted ; for it is eafy to conceive, that, in the fmall quantity of water
the elixir of vitriol, for inftance, is commonly

monly given, that auftere acid can fcarcely get beyond the firft paffages; confidering the delicate fenfibility of the mouths of the lacteals, which muft force them to contract, and exclude fo pungent a liquor. It were therefore a proper experiment to be made, in a deficiency of malt, or when that grain fhall happen to be fpoiled by keeping *, to ufe diftilled water, acidulated with the fpirit of fea-falt, in the proportion of only ten drops to a quart; or with the weak fpirit of vitriol, thirteen drops to the fame mea-fure †; and to give to thofe that are threat-ened with the fcurvy at leaft three quarts of

* Captain COOK told me, that the malt held out fufficiently good for the two firft years; but that in the third, having loft much of its tafte, he doubted whether it retained any of its virtues. Mr. PATTEN, however, obferved, that, though the malt at that time was fenfibly decayed, yet neverthelefs he had ftill found it ufeful, when he employed a larger proportion of it to make the infufion.

† In thefe proportions I found the water tafte juft acidulous and pleafant.

this

this liquor daily, to be confumed as they
fhall think proper.

But if the *fixed air* and acids are fuch
prefervatives againft the fcurvy, why fhould
Captain Cook make fo little account of the
rob of lemons and of oranges (for fo they
have called the extracts or infpiffated juices
of thofe fruits) in treating that diftemper?
This, I found, was the reafon: Thefe
preparations being only fent out upon trial,
the furgeon of the fhip was told, at a conjecture, how much he might give for a
dofe, but without ftrictly limiting it.
The experiment was made with the quantity fpecified, but with fo little advantage, that, judging it not advifeable to lofe
more time, he fet about the cure with the
wort alone, of the efficacy of which he was
certain; whilft he referved thefe *robs* for
other purpofes; more particularly for colds,
when, to a large draught of warm water,
with

with fome fpirits and fugar, he added a fpoonful of one of them, and with this compofition made a grateful fudorific that anfwered his intention. No wonder, then, if Captain Cook, not knowing how much to order of thefe concentrated juices for the fcurvy, but feeing them fail as they were given at this time, fhould entertain no great opinion of their antifcorbutic virtue. It may be alfo proper to take notice, that, as they had been reduced to a fmall pro- portion of their bulk by evaporation upon fire, it is probable they were much weak- ened by that procefs, and that, with their aqueous parts, they had loft not a little of their aërial, on which fo much of their an- tifeptic power depended. If, therefore, a farther trial of thefe excellent fruits were to be made, it would feem more advifeable to fend to fea the purified juices entire in cafks ; agreeably to a propofal which I find hath been prefented to the Admiralty, fome

6   years

years ago, by an ingenious and experienced furgeon of the navy. For, in truth, the teftimonies in favour of the falutary qualities of thefe acids are fo numerous, and fo ftrong, that I fhould look upon fome failures, even in cafes where their want of fuccefs cannot fo well be accounted for as in this voyage, as not a fufficient reafon for ftriking them out of the lift of the moft powerful prefervatives againft the confuming malady of failors.

It may be obferved, that Captain Cook fays not more in praife of vinegar than of the *robs ;* yet I would not thence infer that he made no account of that acid ; but only that, as he happened in this voyage to be fparingly provided with it, and yet did well, he could not confider a large ftore of vinegar to be fo material an article of provifion as was commonly imagined. And, though he fupplied its place in the meffes

of

of the men with the acid of the *four krout*, and trufted chiefly to fire for purifying his decks, yet it is to be hoped that future navigators will not therefore omit it. Vinegar will ferve at leaft for a wholefome variety in the feafoning of falted meats, and may be fometimes fuccefsfully ufed as a medicine, efpecially in the afperfions of the berths of the fick. It is obfervable, that, though the fmell be little grateful to a perfon in health, yet it is often agreeable to thofe who are fick, at leaft to fuch as are confined to a foul and crowded ward. There the phyfician himfelf will fmell to vinegar, as much for pleafure, as for guarding againft infection.

Now the wort and the acid juices were only difpenfed as medicines; but the next article was of more extenfive ufe. This was the *four krout* (four cabbage), a food of univerfal requeft in Germany. The

N   acidity

acidity is acquired by its fpontaneous fermentation, and it was that very tafte which
made it the more acceptable to all who ate
it. To its farther commendation we may
add, that it held out good to the laft of the
voyage.

IT may feem ftrange, that though cabbage hath had fo high encomiums beftowed
upon it by the ancients (witnefs what CA-
TO the elder and PLINY the naturalift fay
on the fubject), and hath had the fanction
of the experience of nations for ages, it
fhould yet be difapproved of by fome of
the diftinguifhed medical writers of our
times. One finds it yield a rank fmell in
decoction, which he confounds with that
of putrefaction. Another analyzes it, and
difcovers fo much grofs air in the compofition, as to render it indigeftible; yet this
flatulence, fo much decried, muft now be
acknowledged to be the *fixed air*, which
makes

makes the cabbage fo wholefome when fermented. Nay it hath been traduced by one of the moft celebrated phyficians of our age, as partaking of a poifonous nature : nor much better founded was that notion of the fame learned profeffor, that, cabbage being an alcalefcent plant, and therefore difpofing to putrefaction, it could never be ufed in the fcurvy, excepting when the difeafe proceeded from an acid. But the experiments, which I formerly laid before the Society, evinced this vegetable, with the reft of the fuppofed alcalefcents, to be really acefcent ; and proved that the fcurvy is never owing to acidity, but, much other-wife, to a fpecies of putrefaction ; that very caufe, of which the ill-grounded clafs of alcalefcents was fuppofed to be a pro-moter *.

* See this remark more at large, in my *Obferva-tions on the Difeafes of the Army*, App. Pap. 7.

AMONG

AMONG other of the late improvements of the naval ſtores, we have heard much of the *portable ſoup*, and accordingly we find that Captain COOK hath not a little availed himſelf of it in his voyage. This concentrated broth, being freed from all fat, and having by long boiling evaporated the moſt putrefcent parts of the meat, is reduced to the confiſtence of a glue, which in effect it is, and will, like other glues, in a dry place, keep ſound for years together. It hath been ſaid, that broths turn ſour on keeping, though made without any vegetable *. Now, whether any real acid can be thus formed or not, I incline at leaſt to believe, that the gelatinous parts of animal ſubſtances, ſuch as compoſe theſe cakes, are not of a nature much diſpoſed to putrefy. But, however that may be, ſince

---

* ' La ſeule matiere qui s'agriſſe dans le ſang eſt la matiere gelatineuſe, &c.' SENAC, Structure du Cœur, l. iii. ch. iv. § 5.

Captain

Captain Cook obferves, that this foup was the means of making his people eat a greater quantity of greens than they would have done otherwife, fo far we muft allow it to have been virtually antifeptic.

So much for thofe articles that have of late been fupplied to all the King's fhips on long voyages, and in which, therefore, our worthy brother claims no other merit than the prudent difpenfation of them ; but what follows, being regulations either wholly new, or improved hints from fome of his experienced friends, we may juftly appropriate them to himfelf.

First, then, he put his people at three watches, inftead of two, which laft is the general practice at fea ; that is, he divided the whole crew into three companies, and, by ordering each company upon the watch by turns, four hours at a time, every man

N 3 had

had eight hours free, for four of duty; whereas, at watch and watch, the half of the men being on duty at once, with returns of it every four hours, they can have but broken fleep, and, when expofed to wet, they have not time to get dry before they lie down. When the fervice requires them, fuch hardfhips muft be endured; but when there is no prefling call, ought not a mariner to be refrefhed with as much uninterrupted reft as a common labourer?

I AM well informed, that an officer diftinguifhes himfelf in nothing more than in preferving his men from wet, and the other injuries of the weather. Thefe were moft effential points with this humane Commander. In the torrid zone, he fhaded his people from the fcorching fun by an awning over his deck; and, in his courfe under the antarctic circle, he had a coat provided for each man, of a fubftantial wool-

len

len ftuff, with the addition of a hood for covering their heads. This garb (which the failors called their *Magellan jacket*) they occafionally wore, and found it moft comfortable for working in rain and fnow, and among the broken ice in the high latitudes of the South.

LET us proceed to another article, one of the moft material, the care to guard againft putrefaction, by keeping clean the perfons, the clothes, the bedding, and berths of the failors. The Captain acquainted me, that regularly, one morning in the week, he paffed his fhip's company in review, and faw that every man had changed his linen, and was in other points as clean and neat as circumftances would permit. It is well known how much *cleanlinefs* is conducive to health, but it is not fo obvious how much it alfo tends to

regularity

regularity and other virtues. That diligent officer was perfuaded, that fuch men as he could induce to be more cleanly than they were difpofed to be of themfelves, became at the fame time more fober, more orderly, and more attentive to their duty. It muft be acknowledged that a feaman has but indifferent means to keep himfelf clean, had he the greateft inclination to do it; for I have not heard that commanders of fhips have yet availed themfelves of the *ftill* for providing frefh water for wafhing; and it is well known that fea-water doth not mix with foap, and that linen wet with brine never thoroughly dries. But for Captain Cook, the frequent opportunities he had of taking in water among the iflands of the South-Sea, enabled him in that tract to difpenfe to his fhip's company fome frefh water for every ufe; and when he navigated in the high latitudes of the

southern

fouthern oceans, he ftill more abundantly provided them with it, as you will find by the fequel of this difcourfe.

Of the hammocks and bedding I need fay little, as all officers are now fenfible, how much it concerns the health of their people to have this part of a fhip's furniture kept dry and well aired; as by the breath and perfpiration of fo many men, every thing below, even in the fpace of twenty-four hours, is apt to contract an offenfive moifture. But Captain Cook was not fatisfied with ordering upon deck the hammocks and bedding every day that was fair (the common practice), but took care that every bundle fhould be unlafhed, and fo fpread out, that every part of it might be expofed to the air.

His next concern was to fee to the purity of the fhip itfelf, without which at-

tention

tention all the reft would have profited
little. I fhall not however detain you with
his orders about wafhing and fcraping the
decks, as I do not underftand that in
this kind of cleanfing he excelled others;
but fince our author has laid fo great a
ftrefs upon *fire*, as a purifier, I fhall endeavour to explain his way of ufing it,
more fully than he has done in his Paper.
Some wood, and that not fparingly, being
put into a proper ftove or grate, was light-
ed, and carried fucceflively to every part
below deck. Wherever fire is, the air
neareft to it being heated becomes fpeci-
fically lighter, and by being lighter rifes,
and paffes through the hatchways into the
atmofphere. The vacant fpace is filled
with the cold air around, and that being
heated in its turn, in like manner afcends,
and is replaced by other air as before.
Thus, by continuing the fire for fome time,
in any of the lower apartments, the foul

air

air is in a good meafure driven out, and the frefh admitted. This is not all : I apprehend that the acid fteams of the wood, in burning, act here as an antifeptic, and correct the corrupted air that remains.

An officer of diftinguifhed rank, another of Captain Cook's experienced friends, mentioned to me a common and juft obfervation in the fleet, which was, that all the old twenty-gun fhips were remarkably lefs fickly than thofe of the fame fize of a modern conftruction. This, he faid, was a circumftance he could not otherwife account for, than by the former having their *galley* * in the fore-part of the *orlop* †, the chimney vented fo ill, that it was fure to fill every part with fmoke whenever the wind was a-ftern. This was a nuifance for the time, but, as he thought, abun-

* Their fire-place or kitchen.
† The deck immediately above the hold.

dantly

dantly compenfated by the extraordinary good health of the feveral crews. Poffibly thefe fire-places were alfo beneficial, by drying and ventilating the lower decks, more when they were below, than they can do now that they are placed under the forecaftle upon the upper deck.

But the moft obvious ufe of the portable fires was their drying up the moifture, and efpecially in thofe places where there was the leaft circulation of air. This humidity, compofed of the breath and perfpirable matter of a multitude of men, and often of animals (kept for a live-ftock), and of the fteams of the bilge water from the well, where the corruption is the greateft; this putrid moifture, I fay, being one of the main caufes of the fcurvy, was there-fore more particularly attended to, in order to its removal. The fires were the power-ful inftrument for that purpofe; and whilft

they

they burned, fome men were employed in rubbing hard, with canvafs or oakhum, every part of the infide of the fhip that was damp and acceffible. But the advantage of fire appears no where fo manifeft as in cleanfing the well ; for this being in the loweft part of the hold, the whole leakage runs into it, whether of the fhip itfelf, or of the cafks of fpoilt meats or corrupted water. The mephitic vapours from this fink alone have often been the caufe of inftantaneous death to thofe who have unwarily approached to clean it ; and not to one only, but to feveral fucceffively, when they have gone down to fuccour their unfortunate companions. Yet this very place hath not only been rendered fafe but fweet, by means of an iron pot filled with fire and let down to burn in it.

WHEN, from the circumftances of the weather, this falutary operation could not

take

take place, the fhip was fumigated with
gun-powder, as defcribed in Captain
Cook's Paper; though that fmoke could
have little or no effect in drying, but only
in remedying the corruption of the air,
by means of the acid fpirits from the ful-
phur and nitre, aided perhaps by fome
fpecies of an aërial fluid, then difengaged
from the fuel, to counteract putrefaction.
But as thefe purifications by gun-powder,
as well as by burning tar and other refinous
fubftances, are fufficiently known, I fhall
not infift longer on them here.

Among the feveral means of fweeten-
ing or renewing the air, we fhould expect
to hear of Dr. Hales's ventilator. I muft
confefs it was my expectation, and therefore, perfuaded as I was of the excellence
of the invention, it was not without much
regret that I faw fo good an opportunity
loft, of giving the fame favourable impreffion

4

fion of it to the Public. If a degree of fuccefs, exceeding our moft fanguine hopes, is not fufficient for juftifying the omiffion of a meafure, deemed one of the moft effential for attaining an end, I would plead in favour of our worthy brother, that by a humiliating fatality, fo often accompanying the moft ufeful difcoveries, the credit of this ventilator is yet far from being eftablifhed in the navy. What wonder then, if Captain COOK, being fo much otherwife taken up, fhould not have had time to examine it, and therefore avoided the encumbering his fhip with an apparatus he had poffibly never feen ufed, and of which he had at beft received but a doubtful character? Nor was he altogether unprovided with a machine for ventilation. He had the *wind-fails*, though he hath not mentioned them in his Paper; and he told me that he had found them at times very ferviceable, and particularly between the

Tropics.

Tropics. They have the merit of taking up little room, they require no labour in working, and the contrivance is fo fimple that they can fail in no hands. But their powers are fmall in comparifon with thofe of Dr. HALES's ventilator : they cannot be put up in hard gales of wind, and are of no efficacy in dead calms, when a refrefh-ment of the air is moft wanted. Should there be any objection to the having them both ?

SUCH were the meafures taken by our fagacious Navigator for procuring a purity of air. It remains only to fee in what manner he fupplied pure water ; another article of fo great moment, that the thirfty voyager, upon his falt and putrid diet, with a fhort allowance of that element, and that in a corrupted ftate, muft account a plentiful provifion of frefh water to be in-deed *the beft of things.*

CAPTAIN

CAPTAIN COOK was not without an apparatus for diftilling fea-water, and though he could not obtain nearly fo much as was expected from the invention, yet he fometimes availed himfelf of it; but for the moft of his voyage he was otherwife provided. Within the fouthern tropic, in the Pacific Ocean, he found fo many iflands, and thofe fo well ftored with fprings, that, as I have hinted before, he feldom was without a fufficiency of water for every ufeful purpofe. Yet, not fatisfied with plenty, he would have the pureft; and therefore, whenever an opportunity offered, he emptied what he had taken in only a few days before, and filled his cafks anew. But was he not above four months in his paffage from the Cape of Good Hope to New Zealand, in the frozen zone of the South, without once feeing land? and did he not actually complete his courfes in the other high latitudes, without the

O   benefit

benefit of a fingle fountain? Here was
indeed *a wonder of the deep!* I may call
it the *romance of his voyage!* Thofe very
fhoals, fields, and floating mountains of
ice, among which he fteered his perilous
courfe, and which prefented fuch terrifying
profpects of deftruction; thofe, I fay,
were the very means of his fupport, by
fupplying him abundantly with what he
moft wanted. It had been faid that thofe
vaft maffes of ice, called *iflands* or *mountains*, melted into frefh water; though
CRANTZ, the relator of that paradox, did
not imagine they originated from the fea,
but that they were firft formed in the great
rivers of the North, and, being carried
down into the ocean, were afterwards
increafed to that amazing height by the
fnow that fell upon them*. But that all
frozen fea-water would thaw into frefh,

* Hift. of Greenland, b. i. ch. ii. § 11, 12.

had

had either never been afferted, or had met
with little credit. This is certain, that
Captain Cook expected no fuch tranfmu-
tation, and therefore was agreeably fur-
prifed to find he had one difficulty lefs to
encounter, that of preferving the health of
his men fo long on falt and putrid provifions, with a fcanty allowance of corrupted
water, or what he could procure by diftilla-
tion. The melted ice of the fea was not
only frefh, but foft ; and fo wholefome, as
to fhew the fallacy of human reafon unfupported by experiments. An ancient, of
great authority, had affigned, from theory,
bad qualities to melted fnow ; and, from
that period to the prefent times, this pre-
judice, extending to ice, had not been quite
removed.

In this circumnavigation, amidft fleets
and falls of fnow, fogs, and much moift
weather, the Refolution enjoyed nearly the

fame

fame ftate of health fhe had done in the temperate and torrid zones. It appears only from the journal of the furgeon, that, towards the end of the feveral courfes, fome of the crew began to complain of the fcurvy ; but the difeafe made little progrefs, excepting in one who had become early an invalid from another caufe. The other diforders were likewife neither numerous nor fatal, fuch as colds in various forms, flight diarrhœas, and intermittents that readily yielded to the Bark. There were alfo fome continued fevers, but which, by timely care, never rofe to an alarming height. Much commendation is therefore due to the attention and abilities of Mr. PATTEN, the furgeon of the Refolution, for having fo well feconded his captain in the difcharge of his duty. For it muft be allowed, that, in defpite of the beft regulations and the beft provifions, there will always be, among a numerous crew, during a long voyage,

fome

some casualties more or less productive of sicknefs; and, unlefs there be an intelligent medical affiftant on board, many, under the wifeft commander, will perifh, that otherwife might have been faved.

THESE, GENTLEMEN, are the reflections I had to lay before you on this interefting fubject; and, if I have encroached on your time, you will recollect that much of my difcourfe hath been employed in explaining fome things but juft mentioned by Captain COOK, and in adding other materials, which I had procured partly in converfation with himfelf, and partly, after his departure, with thofe intelligent friends he alludes to in his Paper. This was my plan; which, as I have now executed, you will pleafe to return your thanks to thofe gentlemen, who, on your account, fo cheerfully communicated to me their obfervations.

O 3   As

As to your acknowledgments to Captain
Cook, and your high opinion of his de-
ferts, you will beft teftify them by the
honourable diftinction fuggefted by your
Council, in prefenting him with this Medal: for I need not gather your fuffrages,
fince the attention, with which you have
favoured me, hath abundantly expreffed
your approbation. My fatisfaction, therefore, had been complete, had he himfelf
been prefent to receive the honours you
now confer upon him. But you are apprifed that our brave and indefatigable Brother is at this inftant far removed from us,
anticipating, I may fay, your wonted requeft on thefe occafions, by continuing his
labours for the advancement of Natural
Knowledge, and for the honour of this
Society; as you may be affured, that the
object of his new enterprize is not lefs
great, perhaps ftill greater, than either of
the former.

ALLOW

ALLOW me then, GENTLEMEN, to deliver this Medal, with his unperiſhing
name engraven upon it, into the hands of
one who will be happy to receive that
truſt, and to know that this reſpectable
Body never more cordially nor more me-
ritoriouſly beſtowed that faithful ſymbol of
their eſteem and affection. For if Rome
decreed the *Civic Crown* to him who ſaved
the life of a ſingle citizen, what wreaths
are due to that Man, who, having himſelf
ſaved many, perpetuates in your Tranſactions the means by which Britain may now,
on the moſt diſtant voyages, preſerve numbers of her intrepid ſons, her *Mariners ;*
who, braving every danger, have ſo liberally contributed to the fame, to the opu-
lence, and to the maritime empire, of their
country* !

---

* Here followed Captain COOK's Paper, which
was preſented to the Society, and is inſerted in part ii.
vol. lxvi. of the Philoſophical Tranſactions ; but, as

the

the fubftance of that publication is now contained in the laft pages of Captain Cook's Voyage, it was judged unneceffary to repeat it here. The only material circumftance of Captain Cook's communication to the Society, omitted in his Journal, is the following extract of a letter which he wrote to the Prefident, juft before his late embarkation, dated Plymouth Sound, July 7, 1776; and is as follows:

'I entirely agree with you, that the dearnefs of the 'rob of lemons and of oranges will hinder them from 'being furnifhed in large quantities; but I do not 'think this fo neceffary; for, though they may affift 'other things, I have no great opinion of them alone. 'Nor have I a higher opinion of vinegar: my people 'had it very fparingly during the late voyage, and, 'towards the latter part, none at all; and yet we 'experienced no ill effects from the want of it. The 'cuftom of wafhing the infide of the fhip with vine- 'gar, I feldom obferved; thinking that fire and 'fmoke anfwered the purpofe much better.'

A

D I S C O U R S E

ON THE

INVENTION AND IMPROVEMENTS

OF THE

REFLECTING TELESCOPE;

DELIVERED AT THE

Anniverfary Meeting of the ROYAL SOCIETY,

November 30, 1777.

By Sir JOHN PRINGLE, Bart. PRESIDENT.

PUBLISHED AT THEIR REQUEST.

A

D I S C O U R S E

ON THE

INVENTION AND IMPROVEMENTS

OF THE

REFLECTING TELESCOPE.

GENTLEMEN,

IT was with equal truth and modefty obferved by our moft worthy Brother, the
Reverend Dr. BRADLEY, in his celebrated
Paper concerning the apparent motion of the
fixed ftars, and the caufes of that deception,
' that the great exactnefs with which in-
' ftruments are now conftructed hath ena-
' bled

' bled the aftronomers of the prefent age to
' difcover feveral changes in the pofition of
' the heavenly bodies, which, by reafon of
' their fmallnefs, had efcaped the notice of
' their predeceffors *.' And indeed it was
upon this liberal principle, the embracing
of every affiftance which could be advantageous to their inftitution, that this Society, from their foundation to this day,
have cherifhed the mechanical arts; nay,
have often affociated thofe artifts that had
invented or perfected inftruments eminently
conducive to the advancement of Natural
Knowledge.

It is a merit of this kind, I would fay a
fignal mechanical improvement, which your
Council have thought proper at this time
to diftinguifh; and they have accordingly
empowered me to announce to you, on
this day of your annual folemnity, that

* Phil. Tranf. vol. xlv.

they

they have adjudged the Prize Medal,
founded on the benefaction of Sir GOD-
FREY COPLEY, Baronet, to Mr. JOHN
MUDGE of Plymouth, Fellow of this Society, on account of his valuable Paper,
' containing directions for making the beſt
' compoſition for the metals of reflecting
' teleſcopes, together with a deſcription of
' the proceſs for grinding, poliſhing, and
' giving the great ſpeculum the true para-
' bolic form *.' Nor do they doubt (con-
ſcious as they are of their zeal for the honour of the Society, and of their attention
to their duty) of obtaining your wonted
approbation, when they ſhall have laid before you the reaſons which moved them to
put this mark of diſtinction upon that communication, amidſt a number of others very
deſerving of praiſe †.

* Phil. Tranſ. vol. lxvii. part i.

† The encouragement of *experimental* improvements, it may be obſerved, was the main object of the
inſtitution of Sir GODFREY COPLEY's Medal.

BUT,

BUT, before I enter upon thefe confi-
derations, allow me briefly to recal to your
memory fome particulars concerning the
invention of reflecting telefcopes, the fubfequent improvements of thefe inftruments,
and the ftate in which Mr. MUDGE found
them, when he firft fet about working them
to a greater perfection, than was attainable
either by the methods which the artificers
thought proper to divulge, or the directions
that had been given by learned writers on
that fubject. Thus you will have under
your view fufficient materials to judge of
the merits of his performance, and of the
equity of your Council in decreeing thefe
honours to him.

' It muft be acknowledged,' fays Dr.
SMITH in his Complete Syftem of Optics,
' that Mr. JAMES GREGORY of Aberdeen
' was the firft inventor of the reflecting
' telefcope; but his conftruction is quite
' different

' different from Sir ISAAC NEWTON's,
' and not nearly fo advantageous*.'

BUT, with much deference to fo refpectable an author, and with all regard to the fame of GREGORY, let us not
forget to do juftice to MERSENNUS, by
acknowledging him to be the man who
is entitled to the credit of having enter-
tained the *firft* thought of a reflector. A
telefcope with *fpecula* he certainly propofed
to the celebrated DESCARTES, many years
before GREGORY's invention; though indeed in a manner fo very unfatisfactory,
that DESCARTES, who had given particular attention to the improvement of the
telefcope, was fo far from approving the
propofal, that he endeavoured to convince
MERSENNUS of its fallacy †. Dr. SMITH,
it

* Remarks upon Art. xxiv.

† Lettres de DESCARTES, tom. ii. printed at Paris
in 1657, lett. 29. and 32. See this point difcuffed by
two

it appears, had never perufed the two letters of DESCARTES to MERSENNUS which
briefly touch on that fubject.

AGAIN, as to his affertion, ' that GRE-
' GORY's conftruction was not nearly fo
' advantageous as NEWTON's,' it may be
accounted for from his having fet it down
early in the compofition of his work, and
forgetting to qualify it afterwards, when,
before the publication, he had received
pretty fure information to the contrary. Or
perhaps he was influenced by the example of
Dr. BRADLEY, who had been a moft fuccefsful obferver, and yet had always preferred
the *Newtonian* telefcope to the other. But
if long experience is allowed to be the final
arbiter in fuch matters, we muft adjudge
the fuperiority to the latter, as that is now,
and has been for feveral years paft, the
only inftrument of the kind in requeft.

two learned and candid authors, M. LE ROI in the
Encyclopedie, under the article *Telefcope*; and M.
MONTUCLA in Hift. des Mathem. tom. ii. p. 643.

GREGORY,

Gregory, a young man of an uncommon genius, was led to the invention, in feeking to correct two imperfections of the common telefcope; the firft was, its too great length, which made it lefs manageable; the fecond, the incorrectnefs of the image. Mathematicians had demonftrated, that a pencil of rays could not be collected in a fingle point by a fpherical lens; and alfo, that the image tranfmitted by fuch a lens would be in fome degree incurvated. Thefe inconveniences, he believed, would be obviated, by fubftituting for the object glafs a metallic fpeculum, of a parabolic figure, to receive the image, and to reflect it towards a fmall fpeculum of the fame metal: this again was to return the image to an eye glafs placed behind the great fpeculum, which, for that purpofe, was to be perforated in its centre. This conftruction he publifhed in 1663, in his *Optica Promota*, a work which in every refpect doth

P   honour

honour to the author. But as GREGORY, as he himself declares, was endowed with no mechanical dexterity, nor could find any workman capable of realizing his invention; after some fruitlefs attempts in that way, he was obliged to give up the purfuit : and, probably, had not fome new difcoveries been made in light and colours, a reflecting telefcope would never more have been thought of, confidering the difficulty of the execution, and the fmall advantages that could accrue from it, deducible from the principles of optics that were then known.

BUT NEWTON, whofe happy genius for experimental knowledge was equal to that for geometry, and who to thefe talents, in a fupreme degree, joined patience and mechanical abilities; NEWTON, I fay, thus accomplifhed, happily interpofed, and faved this noble invention from well-nigh perifh-

4.   ing

ing in its infant ſtate. He likewiſe, at an
early period of life, had applied himſelf to
the improvement of the teleſcope ; but,
imagining that GREGORY's *ſpecula* were
neither very neceſſary, nor likely to be
executed, he began with proſecuting the
views qf DESCARTES, who aimed at making a more perfect image of an object, by
grinding lenſes, not to the figure of a
ſphere, but to that of one of the conic ſec-
tions. Now, whilſt he was thus employed,
three years after GREGORY's publication,
he happened to take to the examination of
the colours formed by a priſm ; and having, by the means of that ſimple inſtrument, made the ever memorable diſcovery
of the *different refrangibility of the rays
of light;* he then perceived that the errors
of teleſcopes, ariſing from that cauſe alone,
were ſome hundred times greater than ſuch
as were occaſioned by the ſpherical figure
of lenſes. This circumſtance forced, as it

were,

were, NEWTON to fall into GREGORY's
track, and to turn his thoughts to reflectors. ‘ The different refrangibility of the
‘ rays of light,’ fays he, in a letter to Mr.
OLDENBURG, Secretary to this Society,
dated in February 1672, ‘ made me take
‘ *reflections* into confideration, and finding
‘ them regular, fo that the angle of reflec-
‘ tion of all forts of rays was equal to the
‘ angle of incidence, I underftood that, by
‘ their mediation, optic inftruments might
‘ be brought to any degree of perfection
‘ imaginable, provided a reflecting fub-
‘ ftance could be found, which would po-
‘ lifh as finely as glafs, and reflect as much
‘ light as glafs tranfmits, and the art of
‘ communicating to it a parabolic figure be
‘ alfo obtained.——Amidft thefe thoughts,
‘ I was forced from Cambridge by the
‘ intervening plague ; and it was more than
, two years before I proceeded farther *.’

* Phil. Tranf. n. 80.

IT

IT appears, then, that, if NEWTON was not the firſt inventor of the reflecting teleſcope, he was the main and effectual inventor. By the force of his admirable genius, he fell upon this new property of light, and thereby found that all lenſes, of whatever figure, would be affected more or leſs with ſuch priſmatic aberrations of the rays, as would be an inſuperable obſtacle to the perfection of a dioptric teleſcope. Here was (if I may uſe the ſimilitude) a diſorder inherent in the conſtitution of this inſtrument, which NEWTON, like a wiſe phyſician, penetrated into, and, by underſtanding the nature cf the diſeaſe, was led to the remedy; one indeed that had been deviſed before, but for a different and a ſlighter ailment, and withal of ſuch difficult compoſition, that the contriver of it himſelf had not been able to prepare it,

IT was towards the end of 1668, or in the beginning of the following year, when

NEWTON,

NEWTON, being thus obliged to have recourfe to reflectors, and not relying on any
artificer for making his *fpecula*, fet about
the work himfelf, and, early in the year
1672, completed two fmall reflecting telefcopes. In thefe he ground the great fpeculum into a fpherical concave; not but
that he approved of the parabolic form
propofed by GREGORY, though he found
himfelf unable to accomplifh it. In a letter
that accompanied one of thefe inftruments,
which he prefented to the Society, he
writes, ' that though he then defpaired of
' performing that work (to wit, the para-
' bolic figure of the great fpeculum) by
' geometrical rules, yet he doubted not but
' that the thing might in fome meafure be
' accomplifhed by mechanical devices*.'

Not lefs did the difficulty appear to find
a metallic fubftance that would be of a

* Phil. Tranf. n. 81.

proper

proper hardnefs, have the feweft pores, and receive the fmootheft polifh : a difficulty, in truth, which he deemed almoft infurmountable, when he confidered that every irregularity in a reflecting furface would make the rays of light ftray five or fix times more out of their due courfe, than the like irregularities in a refracting one. In another letter, written foon after, he tells the Secretary, ‘ that he was very ‘ fenfible that metal reflects lefs light than ‘ glafs tranfmits ;—but as he had found ‘ fome metalline fubftances to be more ‘ ftrongly reflective than others, to polifh ‘ better, and to be freer from tarnifhing ‘ than others, fo he hoped that there might ‘ in time be found out fome fubftances ‘ much freer from thefe inconveniences ‘ than any yet known *.’ Meanwhile here was, as I faid, another ftop ; and the more difcouraging, as it was not, like the former,

* Phil. Tranf. n. 82.

P 4

to

to be removed by ' mechanical devices,'
nor even by any chemical principle that
had been difcovered. That want could
only be fupplied by making repeated trials;
nay, I may fay, as it were, fortuitoufly.
NEWTON therefore laboured till he found
a compofition that anfwered in fome degree, and left it to thofe who fhould come
after him to find a better. The induftry of
Mr. MUDGE has been aiding to that of Sir
ISAAC NEWTON; and the happy affiftant
of that great man has been fo candid as to
acknowledge, that chance did fave him
much trouble, by furnifhing him with a
metallic mixture, which he had reafon to
believe was fitter for the purpofe than any
that had been ufed before, either publifhed
or concealed from the public.

NEWTON having, with his telefcope,
communicated to the Society a full and
fatisfactory account of its conftruction and
performance,

performance, he received from your illuftrious predeceffors fuch thanks as were due
to fo curious and valuable a prefent. And
HUYGENS, one of the greateft geniufes of
the age, and himfelf a diftinguifhed im-
prover of the refractor, no fooner was informed by Mr. OLDENBURG of the difcovery, than he wrote in anfwer, ' that it
' was an admirable telefcope ; and that Mr.
' NEWTON had well confidered the advan-
' tage which a concave fpeculum had above
' convex glaffes in collecting the parallel
' rays, which, according to his own calcu-
' lation, was very great. Hence that Mr.
' NEWTON could give a far greater aper-
' ture to that fpeculum than to an object
' glafs of the fame diftance of focus, and
' confequently much more magnify in his
' way than by an ordinary telefcope. Be-
' fides, that by the reflector he avoided an
' inconvenience infeparable from object
' glaffes, which was the obliquity of both
' their

' their furfaces, which vitiated the refraction
' of the rays that pafs towards the fides of the
' glafs, and did more hurt than men were
' aware of. Again, that by the mere re-
' flection of the metalline fpeculum there
' were not fo many rays loft as in glaffes,
' which reflected a confiderable quantity by
' each of their furfaces, and befides inter-
' cepted many of them by the obfcurity of
' their matter.——That the main bufinefs
' would be, to find a matter for this fpecu-
' lum, that would bear as good and even a
' polifh as glafs. Laftly, he believed that
' Mr. NEWTON had not been without
' confidering the advantage which a para-
' bolic fpeculum would have above a fphe-
' rical one in this conftruction; but had
' defpaired, as he himfelf had done, of
' working other furfaces than fpherical
' ones with due exactnefs*.' HUYGENS
was not fatisfied with thus expreffing to

* Phil. Tranf. n. 81.

the

the Society his high approbation of the late
invention, but drew up a favourable account of the new telefcope, which he caufed
to be publifhed in the *Journal des Sçavans*,
of the year 1672, and by that channel it
was foon known over Europe.

BUT how excellent foever the contrivance was, how well foever fupported
and announced to the public, yet, whether
it was that the artifts were deterred by the
difficulty and labour of the work, or that
the difcoveries even of a NEWTON were
not to be exempted from the general fatality attending great and ufeful inventions,
*the making a flow and vexatious progrefs to
the authors ;* the fact is, that, excepting an
unfuccefsful attempt which the Society
made by employing an artificer to imitate
the *Newtonian* conftruction, but upon a
larger fcale, and a difguifed *Gregorian* telefcope, fet up by CASSEGRAIN abroad as a
rival

rival to NEWTON's, and that in theory only (for it never was put in execution by the author *), no reflector was heard of for nearly half a century after. But, when that period was elapſed, a reflecting teleſcope was at laſt produced to the world of the *Newtonian* conſtruction, which the venerable author, ere yet he had finiſhed his much diſtinguiſhed courſe, had the ſatisfaction to find executed in ſuch a manner, as left no room to fear that the invention would longer continue in obſcurity.

THIS memorable event was owing to the genius, dexterity, and application of a gentleman of this Society, Mr. HADLEY, the inventor of the reflecting quadrant, another moſt valuable inſtrument. The two teleſcopes which NEWTON had made were but ſix inches long, were held in the

* Compare MONTUCLA, Hiſt. de Mathem. tom. ii. p. 647.

hand

hand for viewing objects, and in power were compared to a fix feet refractor; whereas HADLEY's was above five feet long, was provided with a well-contrived apparatus for managing it, and equalled in performance the famous aërial telescope of HUYGENS, of 123 feet in length. Excepting as to the manner of making the *specula*, we have, in the Transactions of 1723, a complete description, with a figure, of this telescope, together with that of the machine for moving it; but, by a strange omission, NEWTON's name is not once mentioned in that Paper, so that any person, not acquainted with the history of the invention, and reading that account only, might be apt to conclude that HADLEY had been the sole contriver of it. But other Papers in the same volume, besides the Minutes of the Society, clearly shew that this worthy Member meant nothing less than

than to arrogate to himfelf any merit in this performance that properly belonged to NEWTON.

IT is known that the fame celebrated artift, after finifhing two telefcopes of the *Newtonian* conftruction, accomplifhed a third in the *Gregorian* way; but, I fhould judge, lefs fuccefsfully, by Dr. SMITH's declaring fo ftrongly in favour of the other. Mr. HADLEY was not lefs communicative than he was ingenious, being ever ready to impart his lights to others: in particular we are informed, ' that he fpared no pains ' to inftruct Mr. MOLYNEUX and the Re- ' verend Dr. BRADLEY ; and that when ' thofe gentlemen had made a fufficient ' proficiency in the art, being defirous that ' thefe telefcopes fhould become more pub- ' lic, they liberally communicated to fome ' of the principal inftrument-makers of this ' city the knowledge they had acquired

' from

' from him*.' Now fuch fcholars, as it is eafy to imagine, foon advanced beyond their mafters, and completed reflectors by other and better methods than what had been taught them.

CERTAIN it is, at leaft, that Mr. JAMES SHORT, as early as the year 1734, had fignalized himfelf at Edinburgh by his work of this kind. The excellent MAC-LAURIN, my dear departed friend, wrote that year to Dr. JURIN, ' that Mr. SHORT, ' who had begun with making glafs *fpecula*, ' was then applying himfelf to improve the ' metallic ; and that, by taking care of the ' figure, he was enabled to give them ' larger apertures than others had done ; ' and that, upon the whole, they furpaffed ' in perfection all that he had feen of ' other workmen.' He added, ' that Mr. ' SHORT's telefcopes were all of the *Grego-*

* SMITH's Syft. of Opt. b. iii. ch. 2.

' *rian*

' *rian* conftruction ; and that he had much
' improved that excellent invention*.' This
character of excellence Mr. SHORT maintained to the laft, and with the more facility,
as he had been well grounded both in the
geometrical and philofophical principles of
optics, and upon the whole was a moft intelligent perfon in whatever related to his
profeffion. It was fuppofed he had fallen
upon a method of giving the parabolic
figure to his great fpeculum ; a point of
perfection that GREGORY and NEWTON
had wifhed for, but defpaired of attaining;
and that HADLEY had never, as far as we
know, attempted, either in his *Newtonian*
or *Gregorian* telefcope. Mr. SHORT, I
am well informed, faid he had acquired
that faculty, but never would tell by what
peculiar means he effected it ; fo that the
fecret of working that configuration, what-

* SMITH's Syft. of Opt. b. iii. ch. 2. Rem. on
art. 489.

ever

ever it was, as far as it then appeared, died with that ingenious artift.

IT is Mr. MUDGE, therefore, who hath truly realized the expectation of Sir ISAAC NEWTON, who, above an hundred years ago, prefaged that the public would one day poffefs a parabolic fpeculum, ' not ac-' complifhed by mathematical rules, but by ' mechanical devices.'

THIS was a *defideratum*, but it was not the only want fupplied by our worthy brother: he has taught us likewife a better compofition of metals for the *fpecula*, how to grind them better, and how to give them a finer polifh; and this laft part (namely the polifh), he remarks, was the moft difficult and effential of the whole operation. In a word, I am of opinion, there is no optician in this great city (which hath been fo long and fo juftly renowned for inge-

Q   nious

nious and dexterous makers of every kind
of mathematical inftruments), fo partial to
his own abilities as not to acknowledge,
that however fome parts of the mechanical
procefs now difclofed might have been
known before by individuals of the profeffion, yet that Mr. MUDGE hath opened to
them all fome new and important lights,
and upon the whole hath greatly improved
the art of making reflecting telefcopes.

To enter into the detail of the ' devices'
(to ufe NEWTON's expreffion), by which
Mr. MUDGE hath arrived at the true parabolic figure, as well as at the other perfec-
tions of this inftrument, would encroach
too much on your time ; and, I may add,
would not be altogether fuitable to the prefent occafion. I have laid before you the
fum of what he hath performed, and declared to you the opinion of your Council,
that without his interpofition the nicety of

the

the art was in danger of being loft; or, at beft, of being kept in the hands of thofe who were not likely to make it public. The character which Mr. MUDGE bears for integrity, would leave us no room to doubt of his being himfelf perfuaded, that he hath in every point brought the great fpeculum of reflecting telefcopes to that degree of perfection which he profeffes: but as authors and improvers, like parents and preceptors, can rarely diveft themfelves of too partial a fondnefs for what is their own, or amended by them, it will be fatif-factory for you to know, that fome of our brethren, the moft intelligent in thefe mat-ters, have frequently difcourfed with Mr. MUDGE upon this fubject; have feen him at work upon the *fpecula;* nay, have exa-mined two reflecting telefcopes (the one of 18 inches, the other of 22) completed by him; and that they are confident he hath by no means exaggerated either what he

Q 2   hath

hath recovered to the body of arts, or what
he hath added to it.

NEED I now fet forth the merit of afcertaining and advancing the conftruction of
the reflecting telefcope, to an audience fo
well apprized of its value ? To you, who
know that of all inventions there are none
fo juftly entitled to our admiration as thofe
which have been fallen upon for enlarging
the powers of vifion ; and that the difcovery of optical inftruments may be efteemed among the moft noble, as well as among
the moft ufeful gifts, which the Supreme
Artift hath conferred on Man ? For all
admirable as the eye came out of the hands
of Him who made it, yet no organ of the
animal frame hath He permitted fo much
to be affifted by human contrivance, not
only for the ufes and comfort of common
life, but for the advancement of natural
fcience ; whether by giving form and pro-

2   portion

portion to the minute parts of bodies (as it
were to the atoms of Nature) imperceptible
before; or by contracting fpace, and, as by
magic art, bringing to view the grander
objects of the univerfe, the immenfe diftances of which had either difguifed their
afpect, or rendered them quite invifible!

IF PLINY, in regard to HIPPARCHUS,
could extravagantly fay, ' *Aufus rem Deo*
' *improbam annumerare pofteris ftellas!*'
what would that pompous hiftorian of
Nature have faid, had it been foretold him,
that in the latter days a man would arife,
who fhould enable pofterity to enumerate
more new ftars than HIPPARCHUS had
counted of the old; nay, who fhould in a
manner verify the vulgar notion of their
being innumerable! who fhould affign four
Moons to Jupiter, and in our Moon (fuppofed by many to have a fmooth and po-
lifhed furface) point out higher mountains

Q 3   than

than any here below! who fhould, in the
Sun, the fountain of light, difcover dark
fpots as broad as two quarters of the earth,
and by thefe fpots afcertain his motion.
round his axis! who, by the varying *phafes*
of the planets, fhould compofe the fhorteft
and plaineft demonftration of the truth of
that fyftem, till then the greateft of para-
doxes, which fuppofed that the earth and
planets revolved about that luminary*! Yet
thefe were but a part of the annunciations
to the world of a fingle perfon, of GALI-
LEO of unperifhing memory! To him his
contemporary, and rival in fame Lord
BACON, afcribed the invention of the *perfpicilla* (for fo they called at firft the telefcopes), and in a figurative ftrain thus expreffed himfelf concerning them: ' With
' thefe *(perfpicilla)*, which GALILEO by
' a memorable effort of genius hath difco-
' vered, we are enabled, as with fome

---

* GALILEI Sidereus Nuncius, fparfim.

' fmall

' fmall failing veffels, to open and keep up
' a nearer commerce with the ftars *.'

NOR did this celeftial commerce ceafe
with the acquifitions of GALILEO, but
hath been extending ever fince the time
that that great man firft turned his glaffes
to the heavens. The famous KEPLER, on
the firft notice, embraced the difcovery,
and, in 1611, the year following the *Sidereus Nuncius* of GALILEO, publifhed a
treatife of dioptrics, geometrically explaining the performance of the *perfpicilla*, and
propofing fome proper improvements of
them. Then came SNELLIUS, DESCARTES,
and other celebrated geometricians abroad,
who applied themfelves to optics, and fuccefsfully cultivated that fruitful branch of
fcience. But whilft, at that period, in
different parts of Europe, men of the firft

* Quæ (perfpicilla) memorabili conatu adinvenit
GALILEUS, &c. Nov. Organ. l. ii. aphor. 39.

Q 4   rank

rank in mathematical ftudies feemed to vie
with each other in promoting not only the
theory of vifion, but the mechanical practice of the inftruments appertaining to it,
and particularly the telefcope; how did
it happen, that, in this country, in the
laft century, which had fo aufpicioufly begun with the lights derived from Lord
BACON and Dr. HARVEY, we fhould afterwards find few traces of any attempt
in that way earlier than the eftablifhment
of this Society? Of this paufe in the
courfe of your philofophical difcoveries,
the diftracted ftate of thefe kingdoms,
under a long civil war, was indubitably
the occafion. For no fooner had we
fheathed the bloody fword, and difplayed
the peaceful olive, than arts and fciences
again fprang forth, and with fo much
vigour, that the advancement made, in
thefe lands, fince that epoch, in optics
alone, may be confidered as one of the

nobleft

nobleſt exertions of the human genius. Not to contend for a general ſuperiority in the publications here on that ſubjeƈt, ſince the time that GREGORY entered firſt into that grand career, to ſilence all competition, I need but mention the *Theory of Light and Colours*; a piece ſo excellent for invention, for judgment in conduƈting experiments, and for drawing the proper concluſions from them, that, had it been NEWTON's ſingle work, it would not only have done laſting honour to himſelf, but to the country that gave him birth. And as to the inſtruments, which of them, let me aſk, hath not been either found out, or ſignally improved, among you? Or what nation is there that hath embraced the arts, and doth not value itſelf on poſſeſſing every piece of this kind of Britiſh workmanſhip? The refleƈting teleſcope I may call wholly yours, both as to the original contrivance,

contrivance, and every ſtep of its advancement : nay, from its revival by Mr.
HADLEY to this day, a ſpace of nearly
threeſcore years, we have heard of no
artiſt, out of this iſland, who hath been
able tolerably to copy, much leſs to add
to, this ſplendid invention.

WHAT acknowledgements, then, GEN-
TLEMEN, do we not owe to our worthy
Brother, who, for above twenty years
paſt, in the uncertain intervals of a toil-
ſome and anxious profeſſion, hath unbent
his mind, not in the periſhing recreations
of the world, but in inveſtigating, with
unremitting diligence, what had been done
but concealed by others, and in making
many ſucceſsful experiments towards perfecting this inimitable inſtrument ! A liberal account of theſe leiſure hours he
hath laid before you in his inſtructive
Paper : a communication, I am perſuaded,

that

that will not only preferve, but fignalize his name in your records, among the very intelligent and ingenuous promoters of the great ends of your inftitution.

A

DISCOURSE

ON THE

THEORY OF GUNNERY;

DELIVERED AT THE

Anniverfary Meeting of the ROYAL SOCIETY,
November 30, 1778.

By Sir JOHN PRINGLE, Baronet.

PUBLISHED BY THEIR ORDER.

A

DISCOURSE

ON THE

THEORY OF GUNNERY.

GENTLEMEN,

AMONG the feveral experiments communicated to the Society, during the courfe of the preceding year, none feeming fo much to engage your attention, as thofe contained in the Paper, intitled, *The Force of fired Gun-powder, and the initial Velocity of Cannon-balls, determined*

by

by Experiments : with much pleasure therefore I acquaint you, that, on account of
the pre-eminence of that communication,
your Council have judged the author, Mr.
CHARLES HUTTON, worthy of the honour of the annual Medal, inftituted on
the bequeft of Sir GODFREY COPLEY,
Baronet, for raifing a laudable emulation
among men of genius, in making experimental enquiries. But, as on former occafions, fo now, your Council, waving their
privilege of determining the choice, have
acted only as a felect number deputed by
you, to prepare matters for your final deci-
fion, I come, then, on their part, briefly to
lay before you the ftate of the *Theory of Gunnery*, from its rife to the time when its true
foundation was laid, in order to evince
how conducive thofe experiments may be
to the improvement of an art of public
concern, as well as to the advancement of
Natural Knowledge, the great object of
your

your inftitution. And if, upon a review
of the fubjeft, you fhall entertain no lefs
favourable an opinion of Mr. HUTTON's
performance, than what your Council have
done, it is their earneft requeft that you
would enhance the value of this Prize, by
authorizing your Prefident to prefent it to
our ingenious Brother in your name.

ARTILLERY (in the large accepta-
tion of the term) took place long before the
invention of gun-powder. We trace the
art to the remoteft antiquity, fince the Sa-
cred Records acquaint us, that one of the
kings of Judah, eight hundred years before
the Chriftian æra, erected on the towers
and bulwarks of Jerufalem engines of war,
the contrivance of ingenious men, for
fhooting arrows and great ftones for the
defence of that city*. Such machines were
afterwards known to the Greeks and Ro-

* 2 Chron. xxvi. 15.

R   mans

mans by the names of *balifta*, *catapulta*, and others, which had amazing powers, and were not lefs terrible in their effects than the cannon and mortars of the moderns. It appears that the *balifta* was contrived to fhower volleys of darts and arrows of a very large fize upon the enemy; whilft the *catapulta*, or *onagra* (as it was otherwife called), was fitted not only for that purpofe, but for difcharging ftones of an enormous weight ; I might fay *rocks*, fince fome of them are reported to have weighed feveral hundred pounds. Batteries compofed of numerous pieces of that kind of artillery, nothing could withftand. Yet, if we are rightly informed, their fole principle of motion confifted in the fpring of a ftrongly-twifted cordage, made of animal fubftances fingularly tough and elaftic. Thefe warlike inftruments continued, not only during the time of the Roman empire, but to the twelfth and thirteenth centuries,

I   turies,

turies, as we find from hiftory; nor indeed is it probable that they were totally
laid afide, till gun-powder and the modern
ordnance, attaining a good degree of perfection, fuperfeded their ufe. The very
intelligent commentator of POLYBIUS* is
of opinion, that the military art rather loft
than gained by the exchange of the *catapulta* for the mortar : but, however that
point may be determined in fpeculation, it
is not likely that the ancient *tormenta mili-
taria* will ever be revived; but that all
nations will keep to the art of gunnery,
and ftudy how to improve it; that is, they
will adhere to a fyftem of artillery, wherein
the moving power depends on the expan-
five force of gun-powder, or of fome other
fubftance of a fimilar nature.

UPON the firft application of this principle to the purpofes of war, nothing per-

* M. FOLARD.

haps

haps was lefs thought of than to affift fo empirical a practice by fcientific rules ; for, however aiding in thefe matters the ancient mechanicians might have been, who, like ARCHIMEDES, had invented or perfected fome of the *baliftic* machines, no praife feemed now due to the mathematicians for either the difcovery or improvement of the new artillery. In fact, we find the practice of the art had fubfifted about 200 years, before any geometer confidered it as one that admitted a theory, or at leaft fuch a theory as was grounded on geometry.

IT feems but juft to trace and commemorate the inventors of the ingenious arts which furnifh matter for difcourfes on thefe occafions; and not only the main inventors, but even thofe who firft turned their thoughts upon the fubject : for, though fuch men may not have produced any thing perfect, yet they may have fuggefted

gefted ideas to others of a lefs inventive,
but of a more executive genius, and who,
unprovided with thefe hints, would never
have made any notable difcovery. I muft
therefore obferve, that the Italians were the
firft who emerged out of thofe thick clouds
of ignorance and barbarifm which had fo
long overfpread this quarter of the world.
They profited by the unhappy fate of Con-
ftantinople ; for, by liberally receiving the
learned emigrants on that diftrefsful occafion, they were largely repaid by their arts
and fciences, and ftill more abundantly by
their language, whereby they were enabled
to read and to tranflate thofe ancient manufcripts, which the Greeks had faved out of
the wreck of their country. The art of
printing, which was eftablifhed foon after,
was the means of quickly diffeminating
thofe treafures of knowledge, and con-
curred with the fall of the eaftern empire,
to form an epoch for the advancement of

learning,

learning, unparalleled in the annals of letters.

THE end of the fifteenth century, and the whole of the sixteenth, were chiefly employed by the Italians in the study and in the translation of the old Greek authors. The geometry of the ancient Greeks, as well as the arithmetic in numbers and species of the Arabians, was cultivated ; but both remained, as it were, sciences by themselves, unassisting to, or at best but weak and reluctant auxiliaries to, the philosophy of the schools : and indeed how could the abstracted doctrines of numbers and quantities be strained to co-operate with a system, in which neither the laws of motion, nor any but the superficial, and often delusive properties of matter, were to be met with ? The genius of the Greeks, all acute and brilliant as it was, had never been properly directed to the interpretation

of

of Nature, and was indeed unfit (as Lord
Bacon pronounced) for a ftudy that. made
fo flow and painful a progrefs, by re-
iterated and varied experiments and obfervations. It was no wonder, then, if the
Mixed Mathematics, as they are called,
defcended to the moderns in a ftate no wife
correfponding to the elegance and certainty
of thofe parts of the fcience which were
elementary and pure ; and that thofe mixed parts fhould have been found defective
and erroneous, in proportion (if I may fo
exprefs myfelf) to the phyfical confidera-
tions that were to be taken into the enquiry. The imperfection of the ancients,
with regard to natural philofophy, was not
perceived at that time : nay, at the period
we are treating of, the learned were firmly
perfuaded of the contrary, and that all that
was wanting to be known concerning the
laws of Nature, and the properties of matter, was to be taken, either directly or by

R 4   deduction,

deduction, from the phyfics of ARISTOTLE. It was not till the feventeenth century was fomewhat advanced, that men of fcience began to liften to Lord BACON and GALI- LEO, the great founders of the experimental and the true philofophy.

MEAN whiie, in the beginning of the fixteenth century, unqualified as the Ita- lians then were for entering upon phyfico- mathematical enquiries*, they neverthelefs made the attempt, and in particular took the theory of projectiles into confideration. Some imagined that a body impelled with violence, fuch as a ball difcharged from a cannon, moved in a right line till the force was fpent, and that then it fell in another

---

* The chief exception that occurs to this general remark, is the rapid progrefs which in that age Co- PERNICUS made in aftronomy; who was not indeed an Italian, but was fuppofed to have profited by his early travels into Italy, which he enlightened after- wards by his admirable difcoveries.

right

right line perpendicularly to the earth. Upon this principle, abfurd as it was, we find one of the earlieft authors grounding his whole theory of gunnery* ; whilft others, diffenting from his hypothefis, admitted only the ftraight line, in which the ball moved for fome time after coming out of the piece, and that other ftraight line in which it fell to the ground ; but afferted that thefe two were connected by a curve line, and that this curve was the fegment of a circle. NICOLAS TARTAGLIA of Brefcia, a mathematician of the firft rank in thofe days, and ftill celebrated for his improvements in algebra, hath been fuppofed to be the author of this doctrine, no lefs erroneous than the former, and for which two of his books have been quoted †.

---

* See MONTUCLA, Hift. des Mathem. vol. i. p. 623.

† Thofe were *La Nuova Scientia*, and *Quefiti ed Inventioni diverfe*.

Thofe

Thefe I have never feen; but, from another of his works, profeffedly written on this fubject, and tranflated into Englifh under the title of *Colloquics concerning the Art of Shooting in great and fmall Pieces of Artillery**, I find him, contrary to the opinion of his contemporaries, maintaining that no part of the track of a cannon-ball is in a right line, though the curvature in the firft part of its flight be fo fmall, that it needeth not to be attended to. But TAR-TAGLIA is far from fuppofing, that the line in queftion hath any relation to a *parabola*, or to any regular curve. It would feem, then, that if this mathematician had at firft been fo far miftaken, as to fancy that fome part of the courfe of a projectile was in a ftraight line, he had afterwards changed his opinion, and was perhaps fingular in what he finally embraced.

* Publifhed at London, A. 1588.

FROM

FROM numerous inftances one would imagine, that, in thofe days, fo far were men of fcience from making experiments themfelves, that they even fhut their eyes againft what chance would have prefented to their fight. For, whoever had minded the roving fhot of an arrow, the flight of a ftone from a fling, or had attended to a ftream of water iffuing from the fpout of a ciftern, might have been convinced, that the path of every projectile was in a conti-nued curve, whatever little he otherwife knew concerning the properties of that one.

BUT had the obfervation of the philofo-phers gone fo far, they had ftill been at a diftance from the truth. They might have perceived a likenefs between the track of thofe bodies in motion and a parabola, and concluded, from analogy, that all projec-iles delineated that curve in the air; but they

they could never have realized their conjectures by mathematical demonſtration,
without previouſly knowing the law of *ac-
celeration* in falling bodies : a diſcovery re-
ſerved for the next century, and for GA-
LILEO*, one of the greateſt ornaments of
it.

IT was he who firſt inveſtigated the effects of *gravity* on falling bodies, and upon
that foundation demonſtrated, that all projectiles would move in a parabola in a non-
reſiſting medium. And, as he made little account of the reſiſtance of the air, the properties of which were then imperfectly known,
he proved that a ball ſhot horizontally
would, in its flight, deſcribe half a parabola ; and, when the piece had an eleva-
tion above the horizon, the ball would de-

---

* He was born in the year 1564; but few if any
of his works were publiſhed till after the year 1600,
and his Dialogues on Motion not before 1638.

ſcribe

fcribe a whole parabola, fuppofing it to fall
on the plane of the battery. By the fame
method of reafoning he fhewed, that whatever the ranges of the projected body, or
the elevations of the piece, were, the ball
would ftill trace that curve line, of a greater or leffer amplitude, by the time it defcended to the level of the place from
whence it came.

THUS far went GALILEO, confining his
projections to the horizontal plane of the
battery : but TORRICELLI, his difciple,
foon after carried the theory farther, by
tracing the fhot to its fall, whether that
place was above or below the plane ; and
ftill found, by geometrical deductions, that
it flew in a parabola of a larger or a fmaller
amplitude, according to the angle of eleva-
tion of the piece, and the ftrength of the
powder.

VARIOUS and numerous had been the difputes in Italy about the laws of motion in general, and efpecially about thofe of projectiles, from the time the mathema= ticians had begun the enquiry, till the publication of the Dialogues of GALILEO on that fubject (a fpace of upwards of a hundred years); but, from that period, fo evident did his demonftrations appear, that all conteft ceafed, and every man of fcience was convinced, that all projectiles moved in the track which he had difcovered. For, as to the refiftance of the air, which he had not pafled unnoticed (as GALILEO himfelf had been the firft, at leaft of the moderns, who ftarted the notion of the weight of the air and the preffure of the atmofphere), yet fo thin and fo yielding did they efteem that fluid to be, that they were affured it could occafion no fenfible, at leaft no material, deviation from that curve. As they had the principle from GALILEO,

GALILEO, fo they believed themfelves warranted by that refpectable author, not to fear, from that caufe, any objection which he himfelf had fuggefted, but had removed. ' Among thefe projectiles,' fays he, ' which we make ufe of, if they are of ' a heavy matter and a round form ; nay, ' if they are of a lighter matter, and have ' a cylindrical form, fuch as arrows fhot ' from bows, their track or path will not ' fenfibly decline from the curve of a para- ' bola *.'

HERE then was the theory of gunnery laid, in appearance, on the moft folid foundation. And thus far the Italians having proceeded, they feemed to have taken leave, and to have committed the fubject to other nations, whofe greater power, or greater ambition, was more likely to make them avail themfelves of the perfection of

* See his fourth Dialogue on Motion.

a mili-

a military art, than their inftructors. We
had reafon, therefore, to expect, that a
neighbouring ftate, intent upon the advancement of the arts and fciences in general, would not fail to give particular attention to thofe that fhould appear moft fubfervient to its grandeur. Accordingly we
find, that our fifter Society of that kingdom
had not been many years eftablifhed, when
an ingenious Member of that illuftrious
Body, not queftioning the foundnefs of the
Galilean principle in regard to projectiles,
in the year 1677 propofed to the academy, as a problem for the improvement of
artillery, how to direct a piece (fuppofe a
mortar) fo as to make the fhot fall where
one had a mind; or, in the common
expreffion, *to hit a mark*, the ftrength of
the powder being given*. This thought
met with general approbation, and fo far

* See Hift. de l'Academ. Roy. des Sciences,
A. 1707.

were

were the academy from raifing any difficulty about the obftruction which the air
might occafion to a body moving with
fo much velocity in it, that we do not find
the making experiments on that head was
confidered by them as an effential ftep to
the folution; but that their principal geo-
meters ftraightway fet about folving the
problem as it had been announced to them,
fome following one method, fome another,
and all upon the fuppofition of a projectile
moving in the line of a parabola. But M.
Blondel, who had been the propofer,
and who more particularly had ftudied the
queftion, compofed a large volume on the
fubject, which he publifhed a few years
after*, under the title of *L'Art de Jetter
les Bombes;* a performance much celebrated
at the time, and that continued in no fmall
requeft long after, as containing, befides

* In the year 1683. See Hift de l'Acad. R. des
Sci. A. 1707.

S   his

his own, the labours of feveral other Members of that Society of the moft diftinguifh-ed merit. So many and fuch hands concurring in framing this work, it was no wonder that the learned throughout Europe were confirmed by it in the *Galilean* theory; and the more, as M. BLONDEL had obviated the only objection they fuppofed could be made to it, the *refiftance of the air*, which he had taken care exprefsly to mention, and fo to combat as to perfuade the reader, that the retardation arifing from that caufe was fo inconfiderable as to be of no account in the practice.

THIS illufion about the fmall or non-refiftance of the air to bodies rapidly moving in it, was fo prevalent at the end of the laft century, and in the beginning of the prefent, that, in the hiftory of the Royal Academy for the year 1707, we find their worthy and moft accomplifhed Secretary,

Secretary, after taking notice of the joint labours of fo many able mathematicians concerned in BLONDEL's publication, ven- turing to fay, ' it did not appear that any ' thing was then wanting for the practice ' of the art (of Gunnery), except perhaps ' perfecting the inftruments for pointing a ' cannon or mortar . . . . . . but that geo- ' metry had done its part, fo to fpeak, with ' regard to practice, &c *.'

BUT far be it from our intention to re - late the imperfections of others, in order to raife ourfelves by the comparifon. Can- dour requires of us not only to acknow- ledge that, in this country, as to the point in queftion, we did not furpafs our neigh- bours ; but ingenuoufly to own that, on the contrary, we were perhaps more liable to exception. For, fome years before

* Hift. de l'Acad. R. des Sc. A. 1707, under the article *Mechanique.*

S 2 BLONDEL's

BLONDEL's work appeared *, a treatife was publifhed by one of our own artille-rifts, ANDERSON (a perfon of eminence in his profeffion), intitled *The genuine Ufe and Effects of the Gun*, in which the author ftrenuoufly fupports the *Galilean* theory; nor do we learn that he was ever contradicted among us, although he undertook to an-fwer all thofe who fhould make objections to it. Nay, when he had an opportunity afterwards of making experiments on the ranges of bombs, and by thefe trials was affured that their flight was not in a para-bola; yet fo far was he from afcribing the deviation from that figure to the refiftance of the air, that he had recourfe to an hypo-thefis, repugnant to all the laws of motion, to falve appearances, and to reconcile thofe experiments with his former doctrine †.

* Viz. in 1674.

† See his treatife *To Hit a Mark*, publifhed in 1690.

AND

' AND did not Dr. HALLEY, fo long the ornament of this Society, communicate, in in the year 1686, a Paper, which he calls *A Difcourfe concerning Gravity*, in which, treating of the motion of projectiles, he fays, that being aware of the deflection from the parabolic curve that might be occafioned by the refiftance of the air, he had made fome experiments, even with cannon-balls, to eftimate the force of that refiftance ; yet conclude, ' that in large ' fhot of metal, whofe weight many thou- ' fand times furpaffed that of air, and ' whofe force is very great, in proportion ' to the furface wherewith they prefs there- ' upon, this oppofition was not difcern- ' ible.' And again, ' though in fmall and ' light fhot, the oppofition of the air ought ' and muft be accounted for ; yet in fhoot- ' ing great and weighty bombs, there need ' be very little allowance made ; and fo ' thefe rules (thofe, to wit, grounded on

' the

' the principle of GALILEO) may be put
' in practice to all intents and purposes, as
' if this impediment (the resistance of the
' air) were absolutely removed*.' Such
conclusions, which we now find to be erroneous, were the less to be expected from
so eminent a person, as they argued too
much haste to finish a theory, that was to
be made subservient to present use.

IT might indeed have been expected,
that men of science, applying themselves to
this study, would have been sooner awa-
kened to the consideration of the great op-
position of the air, by the *Principia* of
NEWTON, published a little after this Paper of HALLEY's†. For in that excellent
work the illustrious author had demon-
strated, that the curve described by a projectile, in a strongly resisting medium, dif-

---

* Philof. Tranf. No. 179, p. 20.
† In the year 1687.

fered much from a parabola, and that the refiftance of the air was great enough to make the difference between the curve of projection of heavy bodies and a parabola far from being infenfible, and therefore too confiderable to be neglected.

HAVE we not then lefs to plead for not attending to the *Principia* of NEWTON in this article*, than the mathematicians of other nations, who, as M. DE FONTE-NELLE obferves †, partly from the difficulty of undertaking that concife and profound work, and partly from a mifapprehenfion of its tendency (which they fancied was to revive the exploded doctrine of *occult qua-lities*), were late in becoming acquainted with it? But it is not fo eafy to account for their inattention to HUYGENS, a known and even then a much efteemed author,

* NEWTON, Princip. Mathem. lib. ii. fect. 7.
† Eloge de NEWTON.

and

and who indeed was fecond to NEWTON alone in fcience and in genius. For he, in the year 1690, had publifhed a treatife on *Gravity*, written in a popular manner, wherein he gave an account of fome experiments he had made at Paris, and in the academy, by which, as well as by mathematical inveftigations, he was convinced of the truth of NEWTON's conclufions, in regard to the great oppofition of the air to bodies moving fwiftly in it; and, by confequence, believed that the track of all projectiles was very different from the line of a parabola*.

BUT, excepting NEWTON and HUYGENS, the learned feemed univerfally to acquiefce in the juftnefs and fufficiency of the principles of gunnery invented by GALILEO, enlarged by TORRICELLI, con-

* Difcours de la Caufe de la Pefanteur. Leide, 1690.

firmed

firmed and reduced to fyftem by ANDER-
SON, BLONDEL, HALLEY, and others;
and fo far were the theorifts, in that branch
of fcience, from fufpecting any defect or
fallacy in thefe principles, that they feemed
rather to reproach the practical artillerifts,
for not profiting more by the inftructions
which they had fo liberally imparted to
them. Nor do we find that an apology
was made for the empirical exercife of the
art, by any author of note in that line,
earlier than the fixteenth year of this century, when M. DE RESSONS, a French
officer of artillery, diftinguifhed by the
number of fieges at which he had ferved,
by his high military rank, and by his abilities in his profeffion; when he, I fay,
thus qualified to bear teftimony, prefented
a *Memoire* to the Royal Academy (of
which he was a Member), importing, that
‘ although it was agreed that theory joined
‘ to practice did conftitute the perfection

‘ of

' of every art, yet experience had taught
' him, that theory was of very little fer-
' vice in the ufe of mortars: that the work
' of M. Blondel had juftly enough de-
' fcribed the feveral parabolic lines, accord-
' ing to the different degrees of the eleva-
' tion of the piece; but that practice had
' convinced him there was no theory in
' the effects of gun-powder: for that, hav-
' ing endeavoured, with the greateft preci-
' fion, to point a mortar agreeably to thofe
' calculations, he had never been able
' to eftablifh any folid foundation upon
' them*.'

Thus, after the theory of gunnery had
exercifed the genius of the learned for
nearly two hundred years, and for almoft
fourfcore of that time had refted on funda-
mentals which had never been contefted, it
was pronounced at once to be almoft en-

* Mem. de l'Acad. R. des Sc. A. 1716.

tirely

tirely ufelefs, and that by one of the moft
competent judges. Now, whether it were
owing to the deference due to the authority
of that experienced artillerift, or to fome
other caufe, I fhall not determine, but obferve, that it appears not from the hiftory
of the Academy, that the fentiments of M.
DE RESSONS were at this time controvert-
ed, or any reafon offered afterwards for
the failure of the theory of projectiles,
when applied to ufe. Nor can I pafs unnoticed the paufe that enfued before any
farther attempts were made to improve the
theory of the art, either upon the old principles or upon new ones, excepting by fuch
authors as feemed ignorant of this tranfac-
tion, and who of courfe were not fufficiently apprifed of the inefficacy of the
properties of the parabola, for directing
practice : or by thofe who were employed
in fpeculatively inveftigating the nature of
the curve traced by a ball in the air ; a

curve

curve which began at laſt to be conſidered as one deviating much from the line of a parabola : or, finally, by ſuch as, having taken notice that NEWTON's ideas had not been duly attended to, endeavoured to avail themſelves of them, and of ſome experiments that had been made by others, for proving the great oppoſition of the air to bodies of ſwift motion ; but without aſcertaining the degree of that reſiſtance, or enriching the art by any practical rules *.

SUCH was the unhinged ſtate of this part of the mixed mathematics, when, within our memory, Mr. BENJAMIN ROBINS took cognizance of it : nor could the ſubject have fallen into abler hands, endowed as he was by Nature with a ſuperior genius and unwearied application. Mr.

* DAN. BERNOULLI, Comment. Acad. Petropol. T. 2. & 3.

ROBINS was deeply verſed in geometry and the doctrine of numbers; but he knew the limits as well as the powers of both, and how inſufficient they were for eſtabliſh-ing any theory where matter was con-cerned, without preparing the way, by finding out the phyſical properties of that *matter*, by many and varied experiments and attentive obſervation. Thoſe who had hitherto treated of the foundation of gun-nery, by being too forward in the applica-tion of their mathematics, had in a manner hurt the credit of that admirable ſcience. They ought to have ſeen the neceſſity of minutely examining every circumſtance which could affect the courſe of a pro-jectile, beſides that of gravity. Mr. Ro-BINS perceived the error of his predeceſſors in that enquiry, and corrected it. Per-ſuaded as he was, from Sir ISAAC NEW-TON's *Principia*, of the great reſiſtance of the air to bodies moving in it, and alſo of

the

the uncertainty of the force of gun-powder, and of the variations in the flight of fhot, occafioned by the unavoidable varieties in the make of it, and in the make of the pieces of artillery which difcharged it; apprifed, I fay, of fo many caufes of aberration, he juftly concluded, that the foundation here was at leaft as much an affair of phyfics as of geometry, and that if the art of throwing bombs had not been advanced by theory, it was not becaufe the art admitted of none, but becaufe the theory which had hitherto been devifed had been both defective and erroneous. He fufpected that moft of the writers on gunnery had been deceived, in fuppofing the refiftance of the air to be inconfiderable, and thence afferting the track of all fhot to be nearly in the curve of a parabola, by which means it came to pafs that all their determinations about the flight of projectiles of violent motion, had declined confiderably from the truth.

truth. But in order to clear this point from every doubt, he found it neceſſary to aſcertain the force of gun-powder, and by that ſtep to eſtimate the velocity of the ſhot impelled by its exploſion. That being done, he proceeded to meaſure the quick-neſs of a muſket-bullet, ſhot out of a given barrel, with a given quantity of powder; and to confirm the truth of his concluſions, he contrived a machine, by which the ve-locity of a bullet might be diminiſhed in any given *ratio*, by being made to ſtrike on a large body of a weight juſtly proportion-ed to it; whereby the ſwifteſt motions, which otherwiſe would eſcape our exami-nation, were to be exactly determined by thoſe ſlower motions that had a given rela-tion to them. The machine was a large wooden pendulum, which ſwung freely, but in ſo ſlow a manner, that its vibrations could eaſily be counted, whatever was the celerity of the bullet diſcharged againſt it.

The

The thought was fimple, ingenious, and inconteftably his own.

HE next enquired into the refiftance made by the air to projectiles of rapid motion, and which he difcovered to be much greater than had been fuppofed by any writer on the fubject; and indeed fo great, that it was manifeft the curve defcribed by any fhot was very different from a parabola, and confequently that all the applications of the properties of that conic fection to gunnery were fo erroneous as to be totally ufelefs. For, by means of this pendulum, placed at different diftances from the mouth of the piece, he clearly demonftrated how much a bullet, flying with a given velocity, would gradually lofe of that motion by the oppofition of the air: therein furnifhing to the learned a fignal and inftructive inftance of the fallacy of the moft fpecious theories, that

do

do not proceed hand in hand with experiments.

I SHOULD too much exceed the juft
bounds of a difcourfe of this kind, were I
to enter more minutely into the fyftem
founded by Mr. ROBINS, confirmed and
improved, as I find, by the labours of feveral of the learned, in foreign parts, of
great celebrity*. I fhall only add, that his
performance well deferves the title he gives
it of *The New Principles of Gunnery*, fince
the author may more properly be faid to
have invented a new fcience than to have
added to an old one. And I believe I may
venture to fay, that no phyfico-mathema-
tical difquifition hath done more honour to
this country, or to the age, than the writ-

---

* It is much to the honour of Mr. ROBINS,
that his writings on this fubject have been tranflated
into foreign languages by men that were the beft
judges of their merit. I need only name M. M. EU-
LER and LE ROY.

T   ings

ings of Mr. ROBINS on this fubject, which have been publifhed, partly by this Society, partly by himfelf, and partly fince his death (in the collection of his whole mathematical tracts) by his learned friend.

BUT though our worthy Brother will ever be celebrated for having been the inventor of the true principles of gunnery, yet it would be too flattering to his memory, to fay he had-carried the theory of this art to perfection. He himfelf was far from entertaining fo high an opinion of his labours : nay, he exprefsly declared, that he left fome material points to be enquired into at more leifure (which other occupations, and his immature death, deprived him of) ; and he much regretted that he wanted conveniency and opportunities for making experiments on balls of a greater weight, than what he had ufed for afcertaining the initial velocity of them.

MUCH

MUCH therefore are we indebted to Mr. HUTTON, who, treading in the footfteps of the deceafed, hath refumed and profecued this laft *defideratum*, and hath fhewn himfelf not unequal to fo difficult an enterprize.

MR. ROBINS, for determining the initial velocity of fhot, arifing from different quantities of powder, made ufe of balls of about an ounce weight; whereas Mr. HUTTON, for the fame purpofe, hath employed thofe of different weights, from one pound to nearly three; or, in other words, Mr. ROBINS made trial with mufket fhot only, Mr. HUTTON with cannonballs from 20 to about 50 times heavier. This was a confiderable ftep gained in a difquifition on that part of the fcience, in which the refiftance of the air, and other circumftances, were not concerned; and where neither analogy alone, nor mathe-

matical

matical deductions alone, nor the two combined, were fufficient for eftablifhing principles applicable to the motion of cannon-
balls, without making a new feries of experiments : and with what labour and
judgment thefe have been performed, you
underftood by the account which Mr. HUT-
TON gave of them in his Paper.

BUT fhould it now be enquired, what
advantages may be derived from Mr. HUT-
TON's experiments, for the advancement of
the art of gunnery, and of philofophy in
general ? I would reply, that, as to the
former, it may be fufficient to obferve, that
though the improvements be only fuch as
can be deduced from the force of fired gun-
powder; yet they are in a higher, more
certain, and in a more general manner,
than what refulted from the labours of Mr.
ROBINS ; who indeed led the way, but
who made, as it were in miniature, thofe
experiments

experiments which Mr. HUTTON hath
executed at large, and which Mr. ROBINS
himſelf wiſhed to have made, as well as
others who have conſidered the ſubject
ſince his time. Now theſe experiments,
though made by Mr. HUTTON with cannon-balls of a ſmall ſize, may neverthelefs
form juſt concluſions when applied to can-
non-ſhot of the largeſt ſize. And ſuch
concluſions inform us of the real force of
powder, when fired, either in a cannon or
a mortar, impelling a ball or bomb of a
given weight; that is, they diſcover with
what velocity a given quantity of powder
drives thoſe projectiles in a ſecond, or in
any other aſſigned portion of time. They
alſo ſhew the law of variation in the velocity, ariſing from different quantities of
powder, with the ſame weight of metal,
and likewiſe that law which takes place
upon uſing balls of different weights. Farther, they point out the advantage obtained

T 3   by

by diminifhing the windage in cannon, and teach us how we may increafe the weight of the fhot in the fame piece, by making it of a cylindrical form, inftead of a fpherical : by this device, a fmaller fhip may be enabled to do the execution of a larger one. And experiments of the fame kind will alfo determine the juft length of cannon for fhooting fartheft with the fame charge of powder.

LASTLY, it is from thefe experiments, or from others that may be made after the like manner, we are inftructed how to anfwer every queftion relative to military projectiles, excepting fuch as depend on the refiftance of the air to bodies moving fwiftly in it. This indeed is a confideration which leaves room for greater improvement in the art, and for conferring frefh honours on thofe, who, like Mr. HUTTON, fhall have opportunities and abilities

5

abilities for continuing and perfecting this
very curious and useful enquiry.

As to the advantages accruing to philofophy from the labours both of Mr. Robins and Mr. Hutton, fpeak they not
for themfelves? The fciences of motion
and pneumatics are promoted by them;
and of what avail their perfection would
be for the farther interpretation of Nature,
you need not be informed. In fine, we
have here before us, in thefe experiments,
the fureft teft of our advancement in true
knowledge, which is, the improvement of
a liberal art, and the enlargement of the
powers of Man over the works of creation.

Some, however, may think, that the
objects of this Society are the arts of peace
alone, not thofe of war; and that, confidering how numerous and how keen the

inftruments

inftruments of death already are, it would better become us to difcourage than to countenance their farther improvement. Thefe naturally will be the firft thoughts of the beft difpofed minds. But when, upon a clofer examination, we find that, fince the invention of arms of the quickeft execution, neither battles nor fieges have been more frequent nor more deftructive, indeed apparently otherwife ; may we not thence infer, that fuch means as have been employed to fharpen the fword, have tended more to diminifh than to increafe the number of its victims, by fhortening contefts, and making them more decifive. I fhall not however infift on maintaining fo great a paradox ; but only furmife, that whatever State would adopt the Utopian maxims, and profcribe the ftudy of arms, would foon, I fear, become a prey to thofe who beft know how to ufe them. For yet, alas, far feem we to be

removed

removed from thofe promifed times, *when nation fhall not lift up fword againft nation, neither fhall they learn war any more!*

———————

MR. HUTTON,

YOU have heard, SIR, the account I have given of the rife and progrefs of the *Theory of Gunnery*, and of your improvement of it ; a recital, which by no means would have done either you or the fubject juftice, had it been addreffed to any other audience than to the prefent. But, as my intention was only briefly to recal to the memory of thefe gentlemen what they knew of this fubject, antecedently to your Paper, and to remind them of the refult of your experiments, I flatter myfelf I have faid what was fufficient on the occafion : being now authorifed by them to deliver

into

into your hand this Medal, as the perpe-
tual memorial of their approbation. And
let me add, Sir, that they make you this
prefent with the more cordial affection, as
by your other ingenious and valuable communications they are affured, not only of
your talents, but of your zeal, for promoting the interefts and honour of their
inftitution.

F I N I S.

ERRATUM.

In the title of the Difcourfe, On the Means of Preferving the Health of Mariners, for 1775, read 1776.

www.ingramcontent.com/pod-product-compliance
Lightning Source LLC
Chambersburg PA
CBHW030859270326
41929CB00008B/493